He Said.
She Said.

Donated by the
Pittsburg Arts and Community Foundation (PACF)

He Said.
She Said.

eight powerful phrases
that will strengthen
your marriage

Jay & Laura Laffoon

BakerBooks

a division of Baker Publishing Group
Grand Rapids, Michigan

© 2010 by Jay and Laura Laffoon

Published by Baker Books
a division of Baker Publishing Group
P.O. Box 6287, Grand Rapids, MI 49516–6287
www.bakerbooks.com

Printed in the United States of America

All rights reserved. No part of this publication may be reproduced, stored in a retrieval system, or transmitted in any form or by any means—for example, electronic, photocopy, recording—without the prior written permission of the publisher. The only exception is brief quotations in printed reviews.

Library of Congress Cataloging-in-Publication Data

Laffoon, Jay, 1961–
    He said, she said : eight powerful phrases that will strengthen your marriage / Jay & Laura Laffoon.
       p. cm.
    Includes bibliographical references (p.).
    ISBN 978-0-8010-7215-4 (pbk.)
       1. Spouses—Religious life. 2. Communication in marrriage. 3. Marriage—Religious aspects—Christianity. I. Laffoon, Laura, 1962– II. Title.
    BV4596.M3L34 2009
    248.8′44—dc22
                                                2009033595

Unless otherwise indicated, Scripture is taken from the HOLY BIBLE, NEW INTERNATIONAL VERSION®. NIV®. Copyright © 1973, 1978, 1984 by International Bible Society. Used by permission of Zondervan. All rights reserved.

Scripture marked Message is taken from *The Message* by Eugene H. Peterson, copyright © 1993, 1994, 1995, 2000, 2001, 2002. Used by permission of NavPress Publishing Group. All rights reserved.

Scripture marked NASB is taken from the New American Standard Bible®, Copyright © 1960, 1962, 1963, 1968, 1971, 1972, 1973, 1975, 1977, 1995 by The Lockman Foundation. Used by permission.

Scripture marked NKJV is taken from the New King James Version. Copyright © 1982 by Thomas Nelson, Inc. Used by permission. All rights reserved.

10   11   12   13   14   15   16   7   6   5   4   3   2   1

In keeping with biblical principles of creation stewardship, Baker Publishing Group advocates the responsible use of our natural resources. As a member of the Green Press Initiative, our company uses recycled paper when possible. The text paper of this book is comprised of 30% post-consumer waste.

green
press
INITIATIVE

This book is dedicated to the pastors and lay couples at countless churches who are a part of our Healthy Marriage Healthy Church Marriage Wellness Initiative and are striving to help marriages grow. And to every couple who understands the joy that comes from investing in your marriage!

Contents

Acknowledgments

We would like to thank Torrey and Grace, without a doubt the two biggest blessings in our lives. Our families, who have shaped us, molded us, and, yes, demented us in just the right ways. Our friends who put up with Jay's heretical questions and Laura's naps, and who know first-hand how little we *really* know about marriage. To the friends old and new whom we have connected and reconnected with via the Internet.

Darren and Janey Goude, who were sent from God at just the right time. All of the wonderful Celebrate Ministries board, staff, and volunteers who fight for marriages alongside us. The incredible professionals at Baker Publishing Group, and the Nashville Agency, thank you all for your expertise and help along the way.

The couples who took our survey and opened their hearts and lives in the hopes of helping others in this journey called marriage.

A Note from Jay and Laura

A s we speak to people about marriage, most are quick to agree that marriage is under attack. They agree marriage is the foundation of family, church, and community. They concur that we should be addressing marriage needs. But, when asked what is being done for marriage, they shake their heads and say "Nothing."

We want to see couples go on the offensive. In this book, we have provided the tools married couples need to fight for their marriage and to help other couples do the same. We introduce eight phrases that will dramatically change the way you and your spouse see one another. Using these eight precision tools, we'll show you specific strategies to strengthen your marriage and our world. A thriving marriage reaches beyond the husband and wife to impact three critical arenas in our culture: our homes, our churches, and our communities.

Our Homes

A recent survey conducted by the Associated Press and MTV asked nearly 1,300 young people between the ages of 13 and 24, "What makes you happy?" MTV expected answers like iPods, TV, Xbox 360, and money. Instead, they received this overwhelming #1 answer: spending time with Mom and Dad!

This survey points to the fact that kids are looking for a home that is a place of joy, peace, and contentment. When couples invest in marriage, homes are built where children and teens thrive.

Our Churches

It is no secret that divorce is wreaking havoc on our homes, but we may not appreciate the effect divorce is having on our churches. An estimated 60 percent of Americans under the age of eighteen do not regularly attend a house of worship. Survey results published August 6, 2007, by *USA Today* show that "7 in 10 Protestants ages 18 to 30—both evangelical and mainline —who went to church regularly in high school said they quit attending by age 23, according to the survey by LifeWay Research." The primary reason they are leaving is that they feel no "connection" to the larger body of Christ. Parents are key in helping teens make a connection to the larger body.

Sadly, most parents today are struggling in their own walks with Christ, which is reflected in their lifestyles and marriages. A survey conducted by the Barna Institute found that four out of ten marriages in the church will end in divorce, affecting one million children each year.

When parents disconnect through divorce, their children often disconnect from the body of Christ. By investing in marriage, we demonstrate to our children that staying connected is important. As a result, our churches will be strengthened.

Our Communities

A report entitled "Marriage and Family Wellness: Corporate America's Business?" from the Marriage CoMission, an Atlanta-based marriage strengthening advocacy group, demonstrates the impact divorces have on businesses. In the year following divorce, employees lost an average of four weeks of work. Lost productivity from marriage and relationship stress costs employers some six billion annually.

Talk about an economic stimulus package! When couples invest in marriage, they become healthier, wealthier, and more emotionally stable employees/employers.

Save Your Marriage, Save the World

You see, we aren't just talking about marriage. This book and the important phrases we explore go far beyond shaping marriage. As marriages change, a ripple effect will touch every home, church, and community. When you strengthen your marriage, you fortify the fibers of our society and impact every aspect of our culture.

A Point of Clarification

The eight needs discussed in this book are needs that exist in every human being. Our experience has shown us that in general four of these needs are more prevalent in women and four are more prevalent in men. While you may be an exception to the rule, this book was written to give couples general ideas about their spouse's needs.

The Power of Words

In his book entitled *The Great Crossover*, author Dan Sullivan shares his theory that there have been four "moments" in the history of words that literally changed the way we live.

The "spoken word" allowed humankind to communicate with each other. Then the "written word" gave humans the ability to record history and thought. Next the "printed word," ushered in by Johannes Gutenberg's amazing machine, brought the written word—and thus education—to the masses. Finally, the "digital word" gave humankind access to the knowledge of the world from the comfort of our laptops.

Our survey of over 1,800 married people reveals that words hold the same immense power in our relationships. In marriage, as in history, words literally change the way we live.

Five Simple Words

Five simple words changed everything that Friday night. Laura and I had worked an incredibly hard week. My head hit the pillow at 11:00 p.m., and I was out like a light. At 11:06, Laura nudged me under the covers. Instantly, an unconscious smile appeared on my face. Assuming she was "making a move," I didn't care how tired I was, this was great news! Pleasurable thoughts raced through my mind as Laura whispered, "Jay . . . someone's in the house!" I was taken totally off guard; I couldn't comprehend what she was saying at first. Now I was wide awake but dazed.

I rolled my head over and peered through half-open eyes, hoping to get a clearer picture of what Laura was saying. She had the covers pulled up to her nose. All I could see were two eyes the size of silver dollar pancakes. She whisper-screamed at me: "Jay, someone's in the house . . . go get himmmmm!"

Two weeks before this famed Friday night, three inmates from the federal prison in Atlanta had escaped: two rapists and a murderer. The rapists were caught the next day, but two weeks later, the murderer still eluded the authorities.

This fugitive's mode of operation was to hide out in the woods of Atlanta during the day. Sometimes he would break into homes while the occupants were at work or school. During the day he would steal food and clothing. At night, he would make his way out of town under cover of darkness. The media was all over this story, tracking "sightings" of him around town. The sightings were making their way right out toward our little subdivision in Snellville.

Earlier in the week, Laura and I had come home to find police cars all over our street. Our neighbors had their home broken into . . . all that was taken was food and clothing.

I shot straight up in bed, my heart pounding out 145 beats a minute, fueled by the instantaneous flow of adrenaline now coursing through my veins. My ears felt as big as satellite dishes as I quietly turned my head back and forth waiting . . . waiting to hear . . . *Thump! Thump!*

Women just don't understand men when it comes to crisis. Young boys dream about opportunities like this, that the newspaper headlines will tell the world of our heroic act of bravery. I knew two things:

This murderer was in my house.

He was going down!

Well, that was the fantasy. Reality . . . I was closer to Barney Fife than Rambo. I fell out of bed, shaking and stumbling around as I made my way to our closet. I did the one thing I told myself I would never do. I got out my shotgun.

Tiptoeing to the door of our bedroom, I chambered a shell. *Chechunk.* In the deepest, manliest voice I could muster, I said, "Laura, call . . . the . . . cops!"

I wanted this murderer to think I was a six-foot-eight, four-hundred-pound gorilla of a man coming after him with an eight-gauge elephant gun. In reality, I was a five-foot-nine pudgy wimp with a 4-10 my grandpa had given me when I was twelve.

We had lived in our trilevel house just over a month and a half. It was our first "home," and we were proud as peacocks—though you couldn't tell by the sparse furnishings. The top floor housed three bedrooms and two bathrooms. I searched all the bedrooms first. The bedrooms with no furniture, no pictures, no nothing. Poking the gun into each room, I simultaneously flicked on the light with the barrel and crouched into the ready position I had witnessed on so many of those TV detective shows.

No one in our bedroom or bath. No one in the first extra bedroom. The second extra bedroom was all clear. I got to the extra bathroom and noticed the shower curtain was closed. As the barrel of the gun whisked back the curtain, my heart raced from vivid memories of that *Psycho* movie. No one in the shower.

I stood at the top of the stairs for what seemed like hours. Five steps would take me down into the living room. If I crept down the stairs, the murderer could ambush me easily. I figured my only chance was a surprise attack. One, two, three . . . *ahhhhhhhh!* I hit the floor, did a perfect roll, and got up ready to shoot anything that moved.

The only furniture we had were hand-me-downs from our parents—the kind of castoffs Salvation Army turns away. In the corner of the living room was an old TV. Really old—the kind that used picture tubes. Remember how those old TVs would glow even after you turned them off? My mind didn't remember; it was telling me there was an alien in the corner of my living room. Luckily, a slow trigger finger saved the life of that old TV. I was ready to blow it away, right then and there.

I checked behind the couch . . . behind the loveseat . . . behind the old, black, duct-taped-together vinyl La-Z-Boy my dad had reluctantly given us. "That's the best chair in the house," he'd said as he pleaded his case to Mom. Mom won . . . Mom always wins.

I was so paranoid, I even checked up the chimney. I must have been thinking of the famed "San Francisco Santa Claus" murders or something.

Since we were living in a tri-level, I still had one more floor to search. A sharp turn around the corner and down five more steps would land me on the lower level in the dining room. I repeated my Rambo jump/roll move down the stairs and nearly concussed my head on a dining room chair. After I regained my footing, I checked the pantry and the fridge. Still in stealth mode, I made myself a quick snack before checking the garage. Nobody!

Coming down off my adrenaline high, I made my way back up to the living room. Passing by the big bay window in our living room, I had a perfect view of our neighbor's front porch. As I stood at the window, I noticed they were having a party. The cul-de-sac was lined with cars. As guests got in their cars to leave, they slammed their doors shut. I picked up the familiar sound I had heard in bed. *Thump! Thump!*

For a moment, I was relieved. I stood there stunned at all the fuss. At that moment, my neighbors came out onto their porch with their last guests of the evening. Their eyes were naturally drawn to my fully illuminated house. We looked like the Griswolds in one of those *Christmas Vacation* movies.

I will never forget the look on that lady's face. Alfalfa from *The Little Rascals* is as close as I can come. Her hair looked like it was standing on end. With eyes as big as dinner plates, she was slapping her husband on the shoulder with the back of her hand. He just stood there, hands in his pockets, slowly shaking his head back and forth.

I realized the problem. All the lights in and out of the house were on, and there I stood in this big bay window, "Wid ma shotgun in ma hand!" I felt like a fool. A big, dumb, stupid fool. Trying to remain calm and cool, I slowly lowered the gun. At that moment, as the cold steel of the barrel hit my stomach, I realized that I was not only standing in this window with a shotgun in my hand, I was standing in this window . . . naked.

Instead of simply dropping to the floor, I spent about twelve seconds trying to hide behind the shotgun. Have you ever tried to hide a 210-pound naked body behind a shotgun? Don't!

Finally, coming to my senses, I dropped to the floor and did the "Bugs Bunny Slither" back up the stairs. I got to the door of our bedroom. "Laura, you are in deep weeds!"

We spent the next day laughing about our paranoia. Heck, we'll spend the rest of our lives laughing at that one.

Those five simple words, "Jay, someone's in the house," altered not only the course of that night but also our marriage forever. I think twice when Laura is convinced she's heard a strange noise. And when Laura nudges me under the covers, my mind takes an obligatory pause before starting its happy dance.

Survey Says

Throughout the book we will present raw data from our survey conducted at Celebrate Your Marriage Conferences. From April 2008 through October 2008 we conducted a survey at our conferences and a more in-depth online survey asking married people to indicate the power of words in their relationship. Quotes that are sprinkled throughout every chapter were taken from our in-depth online survey. We were encouraged, as many people felt free to openly share from their own lives. Our hope is that as you read these quotes, you will identify with others traveling this journey of marriage.

Scripture Says

Scripture continually reminds us of the importance of words. For instance, how did God do his creating? With words, of course! Genesis 1:3 states "And God said, 'Let there be light,' and there was light." The entire creation story is a tribute to words, as our Maker spoke the universe into existence.

Equally amazing is the power of words used by Jesus as he healed the sick, raised the dead, and calmed the seas. Jesus could have performed any of his miracles with the wave of his hand or the nod of his head. Instead, he chose words:

Rise and go; your faith has made you well (Luke 17:19).

Lazarus, come out! (John 11:43).

Quiet! Be still! (Mark 4:39).

Scriptural instruction from Proverbs illustrates the important role words play in our lives.

How good is a timely word! (Prov. 15:23).

The right word at the right time is like a custom-made piece of jewelry, and a wise friend's timely reprimand is like a gold ring slipped on your finger (Prov. 25:11 Message).

The tongue has the power of life and death (Prov. 18:21).

New Testament references provide us with more motivation to think before we speak.

Warn them before God against quarreling about words; it is of no value, and only ruins those who listen (2 Tim. 2:14).

Watch the way you talk. Let nothing foul or dirty come out of your mouth. Say only what helps, each word a gift (Eph. 4:29 Message).

One Woman's Words

Therefore encourage each other with these words.

1 Thessalonians 4:18

While attending a Christian college, I (Laura) dated a Christian man who was studying to go into the ministry. I was sure he was "the one." During the three-and-a-half years we dated, I had many opportunities to be with his family. I loved his mom and dad as if they were my own and of course thought they would be someday!

His parents were very strong Christians, and I respected them immensely. I learned a great deal about real faith from these lovely people. I can vividly remember being at their home, sitting at the kitchen table with his mom. We were discussing my future, dreams for my life, and how I saw the Lord leading me. As I shared with her some of my aspirations, she very quietly and eloquently said,

23

"Laura, I don't know if you and my son will get married, but I do know this: the Lord is going to do great things through you. I firmly believe the Lord is going to use you to feed his sheep." Then she quoted, "If you abide in Me and My words abide in you ask what you will and it will be done" (John 15:7 NASB). She encouraged me to claim this verse and live it.

That day is forever etched in my memory. I will never forget the words she spoke. Her words encouraged me, directed me, and changed me forever.

A Hero

Jim Galvin was my (Jay's) counselor at Honey Rock Camp in northern Wisconsin. During our two-week backpack and canoeing expedition, Jim and I got to know each other as only a camp counselor and a thirteen-year-old boy can.

While most of our time was fun and filled with adventure, one particular afternoon bordered on catastrophe. A fellow camper tripped and—with the weight of his thirty-pound backpack on his thirteen-year-old frame—lost his balance, falling headlong into a hornets' nest. Immediately, hornets were everywhere. As campers scattered like marbles dropped on the floor, all I could see was this poor kid unable to get up because he was being stung repeatedly by hornets. Without thinking, I lunged toward him, pulled him from the nest, and literally swept him and his backpack away. To say it was the mother of all adrenaline rushes would be an understatement!

Twelve years later I was at a Youth for Christ staff training event. My small group leader was none other than my old camp counselor, Jim Galvin. Jim said he wanted to begin our time together talking about heroes because our work with Youth for Christ, and evangelizing the lost, was spiritually heroic. Not because of our actions, mind you, but because of the Hero that paid the price for our sin.

Jim began to recount a story from his days as a counselor at Honey Rock Camp. Without using names, he vividly retold the story of a boy, a hornets' nest, and a hero. He then turned to me and in front of our small group, pointed to my face and said, "Jay Laffoon is that hero." I cannot describe the emotions that were running through me at that moment. The act I performed when I was thirteen years old was simply a reaction. Jim's *words* changed my life.

Healing Words

There is healing in the words of the wise.

Proverbs 12:18 The Message

Jay and I had a whirlwind romance. Jay asked me to marry him a mere ten days after we were set up on a blind date. We went with our friends to a baseball game.

Since neither of us were big fans of "America's pastime," we did more talking than watching. Our disinterest in the game, combined with the fact that the couple who set us up were new-lyweds and couldn't keep their hands off each other, gave us the opportunity to share a lot of details that night.

We talked about our lives, family, education, and dreams. I remember telling Jay that my dad had passed away a year earlier and we were coming up on the one year anniversary of his death in exactly a week. That next week, Jay and I ended up at the same Bible study. When Jay arrived, he came over to where I was sitting and asked, "How are you?" "Fine," I replied. Then he said, "No, I mean, how are you *today*?" I couldn't believe he remembered. I mean, the Bible study started at 7:00 p.m. and I myself hadn't thought once about my daddy's death that day. Jay's words, spoken in genuine love and care, drew my heart to his in a way I cannot describe.

Jay's love for me, expressed in a simple question, sent me reeling head over heels.

More Than Words

Often in marriage it's not just the words (text) that convey a message, but also the tone (subtext) with which the words are uttered. Our friend Chad reminded us of an exercise performed in college drama classes involving text and subtext. "Text" is the *words spoken* and "subtext" is the *underlying meaning* behind the text. For example, a student might be assigned to say the words "I love you" to others in the class. The assignment might be to say the same "text" with three different "subtexts": to one classmate, "you disgust me"; to another, "I'm very nervous saying this"; and yet another, "I mean this forever."

When I (Jay) say "I suppose," spoken with an emphasis on the "*ose*" and a sigh at the end, this is really not the enthusiastic answer Laura is looking for when she asks if I want to go to the mall. I never want to go to the mall, and Laura knows this; but there are times she's not going to the mall to shop, she just wants my company.

Almost without hesitation she'll gently come back with, "You don't *have* to go if you *really* don't want to." Her tone, and the emphasis on "have" and "really," speak volumes and tell me that we are no longer talking about a trip to the mall. We have transitioned to a weightier discussion about my commitment to her need for quality time . . . and my subsequent need for the good mood she's in when I do spend time with her.

I didn't begin to realize how important tone of voice was until I began disciplining our son, Torrey, as a toddler. I could literally make him cry with a stern word. The tone in my voice and "the look" communicate depths beyond the mere words I use.

On many occasions throughout our marriage, Laura has asked, "Why do you think I'm stupid?" "I don't think you're stupid" comes my quick reply. "Well, the tone in your voice certainly implies that I'm a downright idiot." You see, I can ask a simple question like, "Why are you doing *that*?" The words are harmless enough. But, my emphasis, tone, and facial gestures communicate to Laura that I'm really not asking a question at all. I'm letting her know that whatever she is doing, I think she is going about it in absolutely the wrong way.

Most marriages have at least one person with a tone of voice issue. It could be like mine, with the underlying implied message. Or it could be the "quarrelsome wife" Solomon wrote about in Proverbs 27:15: "A quarrelsome wife is like a constant dripping on a rainy day." I am so glad my wife is not quarrelsome. So in gratitude, I work diligently to manage my tone of voice.

Timing Is Everything

We men really have no right to say "We just had a baby!" Let's be honest—we have very little to do with the whole process. From the moment after conception until delivery, we're just a support system.

When Laura became pregnant with Torrey, we guarded our excitement at first. Laura had already experienced one miscarriage, and we didn't want to raise our hopes too high too soon.

The further along in the nine-month process we got, however, the more our joy understandably grew.

We busied ourselves creating a nursery and picking out names. We took the perfunctory Lamaze class and I learned the vital role I would play in the birth of our baby. I was ready!

Two full weeks before Laura's due date, she spent the night on the living room couch with what she described as "some pain in my lower back." Oblivious to the fact she had spent the night out of our bed, I flippantly remarked what a good night's rest I had. That went over well.

Though neither one of us thought she was in labor, Laura's significant pain merited a trip to the doctor. I threw my gym bag into the car, fully expecting to play basketball over lunch. Off we went.

When we arrived at the doctor's office, Laura was cheerfully greeted by three nurses, and I was unceremoniously ignored. Soon the nurses were asking Laura questions in rapid-fire succession. In unison they sung out, "You're in labor!" They looked at me, recognized my ineptitude, and said, "We'll get her admitted to the hospital; you just take care of yourself!"

Laura was admitted at 9:30 a.m. She gave birth to Torrey at 3:19 p.m. This six-hour window of time allowed for friends and family to stop by and wish Laura well. Meanwhile, I was feeding her ice chips and placing cool compresses on her forehead—anything and everything I could to make her comfortable as she gave birth to our son.

Around 2:00 p.m. the contractions started getting closer together. By this time, I was exhausted. I mean, all that coaching, and ice chips, and refreshing cool compresses . . . come on! A man can only hold on for so long.

So, I was taking a much-needed break, talking with Laura's sister Sandy and our friend Sue Stack. We were at the foot of the bed—and, yes, we were laughing about something—when, out of nowhere, a tepid washcloth hit me right in the face. Splat!

We turned to Laura, who said, "Giving birth here . . . could you freshen my compress?" To this day, Sandy and Sue laugh when they recall that washcloth clinging to my face.

Around 3:00 p.m. Doc Hall came in. "It's time." One thing you need to know about me is that I am easily excitable. I get downright giddy over a fresh cup of coffee. I explode with anticipation over certain TV shows. And if a buddy asks me to play golf, I have a hard time sleeping the night before. When I heard Doc utter the words "It's time," I couldn't contain myself.

I knew my position: next to Laura's left ear. I knew my word: push! And I knew I was going to say that word better than anyone had ever said it before.

December 7, 1990, at 3:19 p.m., Torrey James Laffoon entered this world. Later that night Laura told me she had never felt so loved—so cared for, so connected to another human—than when I was screaming that single word *push*. I had redeemed myself. Sometimes the right word, at the right time, makes all the difference.

Sticks and Stones . . .

> No one has a finer command of language than the person who keeps his mouth shut.
>
> Sam Rayburn

As a young youth minister, twice I had words come out of my mouth that had a lasting impact—and they haunt me to this day.

Laura and I had our first ministry experience together with Youth for Christ in Atlanta, Georgia. We were assigned the task of starting Campus Life clubs in Gwinnet County high schools. At that time, Gwinnett County—suburbia north and east of I-285, Atlanta's "perimeter"—was the fastest-growing county in the United States. We jumped in with both feet.

Our flagship club was at Brookwood High School. In our first year of ministry, we were busting at the seams with kids coming to our events. As a result of getting to know a lot of the kids, we had a strong core group of student leaders. One of those leaders was a freshman named Steve. Steve was a great kid who had a lot of enthusiasm for the ministry we were doing on campus. But Steve was one of those kids who easily got under my skin. He constantly teased me about being heavy. Growing up, I was always the "husky" kid. As our friend Thor Ramsey says, "If you are a heavy person, and have been a heavy person all your life, then you are not fat—you are *maintaining*." I have since come to grips with my "huskiness," but as a twenty-five-year-old youth minister, I had not.

At one of our events, where there must have been food present, Steve began riding me like a swaybacked mule. I reached my breaking point. I put an arm around Steve's shoulder and said, "Yep, Steve, I'm heavy. The good news is I can change that. Steve, you are ugly, and that will never change." We never saw Steve at another event.

A few years later, I was the featured speaker at a winter snow camp. The sponsor who had brought me in, Trip Butler, had used me numerous times. I was convinced my phone number would be on his "featured speaker speed dial" for years to come. On Saturday afternoon, we were playing some silly game in the snow. I can't even remember the name of the game or how it was played, but it *was* a game, which meant competitive Jay wanted to win. In the heat of competition, one of the counselors made an illegal move and subsequently knocked me out of the game. Angered and frustrated by his cheating, I yelled at the top of my voice, in front of dozens of students, and called him a name I can't bring myself to put into print. I never spoke again for Trip Butler.

Whoever coined the phrase "Sticks and stones may break my bones, but words will never hurt me" obviously never experienced the searing pain of hearing—or saying—words that hurt.

Why Are You Such a Butt?

Careful words make for a careful life; careless talk may ruin everything.

Proverbs 13:3 The Message

People often get the impression that folks who write about marriage must have the whole thing figured out. Nothing could be further from the truth; no one has marriage figured out, and quite honestly we all stink at marriage from time to time. In fact, in our house, more often than we'd like to admit.

It was a month before Thanksgiving and all our relatives had decided to come to our house for Thanksgiving dinner. Laura was really beginning to enjoy cooking and was excited at the prospect of preparing a feast fit for a Norman Rockwell painting. She informed me there was only one issue: the stove. Our house still had the original stove, nearing twenty years old. One of the burners didn't work, another was temperamental, and the oven didn't heat evenly. *We* decided that a new oven needed to be purchased in order for Thanksgiving to be "perfect."

31

I was a reluctant participant in the purchase but relented with one caveat: Laura would arrange for the disposal of our old stove. She cheerfully agreed. When the new stove arrived, the old stove was placed out in the garage and I was assured it would be taken care of at a later date. Thanksgiving came and went. Christmas came and went. Easter came and went. Memorial Day came and went. The stove stayed and stayed . . . taking up valuable space in my, er, our garage.

One Saturday in June, I was cleaning out the garage—trying to make room for our cars to be parked inside—when that blasted stove caught my eye. I'd had enough. I was dirty, sweaty, and frustrated. I burst into the house and shouted at Laura, "When are *you* going to get that stupid stove out of *my* garage?"

I don't know the full content of the heated dialogue that took place next, but it ended with Laura grabbing our fourteen-year-old son Torrey and saying, "Come on. You're going to help me get rid of this stove." I watched—and laughed—in morbid delight as the two of them wrestled with the appliance, trying to maneuver it into the back of our minivan. "Stop it, stop it," I finally said. "I'll go to Dad's and get his trailer. I'll take the stove to Goodwill."

By this time Laura was dirty, sweaty, and frustrated. She said, "Fine, but I just have one question. Why do you have to be a *butt* about things like this?" Now both of us were hurt, angry, and frustrated. We spent the rest of the day working at various projects around the house without saying another word to each other. It was one of those days when the silence was deafening.

We had successfully avoided each other most of the day. That night we had dinner plans with our pastor, Steve Wimmer. We enjoyed fresh grilled hamburgers and a delicious fruit salad. After dinner I began to tell the story of our "fun" day around the house. Steve and his wife, Dawn, were laughing as I imitated my poor wife and son and their futile attempt to load the stove into the van.

When I finished, our hosts could hardly contain themselves. Steve said, "Follow me." He led us in to their garage to see—you guessed it—a stove. The Wimmers proceeded to tell us that they had a similar argument about their stove that very day.

As we headed back out to their patio for some ice cream, Dawn said to Laura, "Just one piece of advice, hon. Never ask the question, 'Why are you such a butt?' Instead make it a statement, 'You are a butt!' That way they don't have an opportunity to respond."

While Laura, the Wimmers, and I can look back on this day and laugh, often this type of discourse—filled with words that hurt—drives a wedge into a marriage. That wedge, left unattended, gets buried deeper and deeper, forming a rift that can take months or years to repair.

Marriage According to Golf?

Billy Watchtorn was the PGA pro at Pine River Country Club in our hometown of Alma, Michigan, for a number of years. Billy's laid-back personality and wry smile was a perfect fit for our small community. His knowledge of golf and ability to teach made him a favorite with high handicappers and scratch players alike.

One day I was talking with Billy about my friend Scott Davis, a very good player. I was sharing with Billy my amazement at the size of the divots Scott produces. Seriously, some of his divots are so big they resemble beaver pelts! (A divot is the piece of sod that is "cut" out of the ground by the club when one properly hits down on the golf ball.)

Without hesitation, Billy went into a lesson on the importance of properly replacing a divot. If the divot is replaced immediately, the ground will heal in as little as twenty-four hours. However, if an hour passes before the divot is replaced, it can take up to a week for the ground to heal. Finally, if that divot sits for a day, it becomes unable to reattach its root system. The ground can take up to a month to grow new grass.

Harsh words spoken in marriage leave scars in our spouse much like the golf club leaves a scar in the ground upon contact. We have received countless comments over the years on how "replacing verbal divots" has helped marriages tremendously.

When we realize that the words of our mouth or the tone of our voice has "cut" our spouse, then the sooner we address the issue, the more quickly the cut heals. When we admit our mistake immediately, the healing begins immediately. However, if we wait for an hour or two, often the healing takes longer. If we wait days—or weeks—to address the words of our mouth, the scar can be permanent.

No one gets this right 100 percent of the time. The key is to pay attention to the signs our spouses give that indicate our words have had a negative impact. I still deal with tone of voice issues, just like I'm still learning how to hit that low hooking three wood. But, just like I do with my golf game, I'm listening to the Pro and attempting to improve my "swing" when it comes to the words I have for Laura.

Let's Rewrite History

Adolf Hitler said, "If you repeat a lie often enough, people will believe it is true." History shows us the unfortunate power of that principle. Likewise, if you repeat the truth often enough, people will believe it is true. Truth will change their lives forever.

This book is about powerful words that speak the truth to your spouse in ways they will understand. We all know men and women think differently. They speak differently and hear differently too. We are going to unlock the mystery behind your spouse's words as we share eight phrases that will revolutionize communication in your marriage. But before you turn the page, we want to tell you that these words alone will not improve your relationship. Rote repetition of these powerful phrases will not automatically make your marriage better. Communication is more than the simple "mechanics" of human conversation.

Discovering the phrases that will change your relationship with your mate is important. But equally important is speaking those phrases with your heart. Make sure your spouse hears your heart as well as your words. Marriage is about revealing to your spouse the depth of who you really are and how you really feel.

That truth will change your marriage forever.

Questions for Reflection

- We have introduced the power of words in this first chapter. Take a moment and reflect on a time when words
  - encouraged or inspired you
  - hurt or harmed you
  - made you laugh
- In this book we are going to discuss four phrases that a wife needs to hear from her husband and four phrases that a husband needs to hear from his wife.
  - She needs to hear:
    - I love you
    - I respect you

- I desire you
- I cherish you
- He needs to hear:
  - I am proud of you
  - I need (*blank*) from you
  - I want you
  - I believe in you
- At first glance, which of these phrases do you need to hear the most? The least? Why?
- At first glance, which of these phrases do you think your spouse needs to hear the most? The least? Why?

She Needs to Hear
"I Love You"

Might as well face it, you're addicted to love.

Robert Palmer, 1985

We have a good friend Gordy, who claims that he says "I love you" to his wife once a year on their wedding anniversary. His rationale is that he said it on their wedding day and to say it more often than once a year would cheapen the expression. When you get to know Gordy and how he was brought up, you realize that he loves his wife deeply; he just communicates his love in nonverbal ways.

Gordy is not the only one who reserves his verbal expressions of love for special occasions. Below are two women who express their need to hear those three special words.

> He does his best to communicate that he loves me by doing, doing, and more doing. Well, that does not work! I have even pointed this out to him, and we just laugh as he is programmed this way and only our great God will be able to change that. So I know he loves me, but the communication part is not there.

> Hmmmmm. It's been a very long time. He was put on the spot to express to me his feelings by a third party, and he said it.

Hearing Is Believing

For women, being shown they are loved is not an adequate substitute for being told they are loved. Hearing the words *I love you* has deep meaning. We can't put our twelve-year-old daughter Grace to bed at night without a chorus of *I love yous*. Something inside

Grace just can't hear it enough. For most women, the same holds true. Hearing those words makes strong connections from their heads to their hearts. Here are six different women testifying to the power of those words.

> For years he would not say or write in a card I Love You. I would always cry about it. However, when he DID start saying I love you (and writing it) it meant a lot to me.

> He says it three to four times a day. He is typically very good at this.

> He tells me how much he misses me and would love to snuggle up, feeling my body and going to sleep. He tells me all the time that he loves me and misses me so much.

> He does a lot. Sometimes he will slip me text messages or email. Every morning before he leaves and at bedtime after we pray together.

> Every day. We start our day and end our day with "I love you."

> Every day after we talk on the phone.

Seeing Is Believing

While saying the words *I love you* is absolutely essential to wives, acting out the phrase is incredibly important too. Because every woman is different, the challenge is finding out what action speaks loudest to *your* wife. Here are three examples of how men communicate *I love you* to their wives.

> My love language is "acts of service." He tells me that he loves me in many ways. He cares for me when I'm sick, runs errands, does

dishes, rubs my back . . . lots of little acts of love. He also says the words "I love you" and buys me cards and presents.

Last night he brought me my favorite kind of chocolate bar from the grocery store, without me asking for it. That is one of his sweet little ways of telling me "I love you"—ways that mean the world to me.

When he puts the things back in the fridge after supper. He brings me roses sometimes. He keeps my car running good. He gently strokes my face when I lay in his lap. He goes to work every day. He makes me a fire before he goes out to the barn. He loves our kids and gives himself readily. He wanted to be a part of parent teacher meetings. He calls me from work or when he travels. He just *tells* me and wraps me in his arms. He's a honey, that's for sure. Buys wonderful cards. Puts up with me!

While candy and flowers work for some, for others it's help around the house. For some it's time alone, and for others it's cuddling late at night. Most likely for your wife it's a combination of a few. The challenge is to know what you are looking for.

The Eye of the Hunter

Our good friend Ken Davis is a very good hunter. In his seminar "Dynamic Communicators Workshop," he uses an example from hunting when he talks about gathering good illustrations for your presentations. Ken will flash a picture on the screen and ask the audience, "How many deer do you see in the picture?" The untrained eye will notice one, or maybe two. When Ken states there are five deer in the picture, most shake their heads in disbelief.

Then, Ken describes what an experienced hunter looks for in the woods: a horizontal line (there are no horizontal lines in the woods except fallen trees and the backs of animals) or a patch of white (deer's tail) in an otherwise green forest. As Ken tells his students what to look for, suddenly it's as if the deer pop off the screen.

Just like a hunter, your job is to figure out what actions will speak *I love you* to your wife. Like the deer on the screen, your wife's signs will pop out at you when you know what you are looking for.

It's been a long time since we went on a date.

Boy, flowers would sure brighten up this kitchen.

Do you like my new haircut?

Five Sensing

"Five Sensing" is another technique taught at Ken Davis's seminar. C. McNair Wilson, an instructor on Ken's staff, shares with attendees how good communicators "Five Sense" the environment of a room before they speak.

To "Five Sense" a room, the presenter enters the room before anyone else and asks questions based on our five senses: sight, smell, touch, hearing, and taste.

How does the room **look?**
Is it bright and well lit?

How does the room **smell?**
Are there any unpleasant odors?

How does the room **feel?**
What is the ambient temperature? Are there any drafts?

How does the room **sound?**
Does it have good acoustics or does it echo like a canyon?

How does the room **taste**?

Are participants going to be eating or drinking?

We frequently speak in the theater at the Grand Hotel on Mackinac Island, and it is a perfect example of how we Five Sense a room.

Sight: With its salmon-and-white-striped walls, large stage, and big red curtain, the theater looks like a giant version of a Barbie Dreamland Playhouse. Barbie's Playhouse is understandably off-putting to most men on their first visit. There's not a lot we can do about how it looks, so let's move on to some senses we can control.

Smell: Grand Hotel is a summer-only hotel. After it has been shut up for the winter, the theater can often smell musty. We bring in fresh flowers or plug in air fresheners to eliminate that odor.

Touch: We intentionally put the chairs close and keep the temperature a bit cool so that couples naturally feel a desire to cuddle when they arrive.

Hearing: When the participants enter the theater, they hear upbeat music. Love songs from years gone by spark memories of young love.

Taste: Complimentary coffee, tea, and lemonade refresh each couple as they enter the theater.

Almost imperceptibly our senses have a profound impact on our mood, attitude, and sense of well-being. When a presenter takes the time to analyze these senses, how he then chooses to alter the environment can either enhance or inhibit the communication process. Similarly, when you Five Sense your wife, you have the opportunity to enhance your communication of *I love you*. Don't understand? Keep reading . . .

Sensitive versus Emotional

As a guy, you are probably wondering what all the fuss is about our senses. Before we explain how to make Five Sensing work for you, let's take a minute to explain why it will work for you.

Most everyone would agree with the statement that, in general, women are more sensitive than men. Immediately our minds travel to the fact that, generally speaking, women cry more easily than men, laugh more quickly than men, and are more quickly attuned to a hurt or crying child than men. We generally equate *sensitive* with *emotional*. While women may also be more emotional than men, that is not what *sensitive* means.

The word *sensitive* has the same Latin root (*sensus*) as the word *senses*. When we say women are generally more sensitive, we are saying that women are more acutely aware of their senses. Not surprisingly, one comment heard time and again from women in our survey is that they wish their husbands would become more aware. Guys, when you Five Sense your wife, increased awareness will be a natural result! Five Sensing your wife is a powerful way to communicate *I love you*. Still don't understand? Keep reading . . .

Getting Started

Men, I (Laura) understand that the only thing on your mind after a long day at work is to relax. You want to sit down, take a load off, and eat some dinner. Trust me; your wife would love to do that too. Instead, she'll fix dinner and take care of the house and kids. So, do me this favor. While driving home, remind yourself that the moment you walk in the door, you need to Five Sense the atmosphere in your home.

I do this with my kids every day when they walk in the door from school by asking myself a few simple questions.

What is the countenance on their face?

What does their body language tell me?

Are they running in the house smiling and laughing, or do they look like they have lost their best friend?

I can tell a lot about how school went simply by observing how they walk in the door. A husband can tell a lot about how a wife's day went simply by observing the atmosphere in the home when he walks through the door. Believe me when I tell you that how her day went, whether at work or at home, will affect the atmosphere! Five Sensing your wife won't take long, I promise. But the result will be a more peaceful evening, every evening.

How Does Your Wife Look?

How your wife looks, both her body language and her outward appearance, will tell you a great deal about how her day went and how she is feeling about herself as a woman.

If your wife is smiling and laughing when you walk through the door, then you're good to go . . . to go kick up your feet and catch up on the news! However, if you observe frowning and growling, tread lightly. Take a low-key approach as you offer your services. "Can I help you with dinner?" An even better question might be, "Where would you like to go for dinner?"

While this is a great starting point, it won't be the answer for every woman. Remember, we are complex creatures. What works for one wife won't necessarily work for another. The reality is this: going out to dinner might work for one woman, where a simple hug and a shoulder to lean on works for another. I (Laura) can only help men so much; then they must go it on their own! But I will give this encouragement: most women will welcome a period of trial and error. You may not get it right on the first try, but your wife will appreciate that you are making an effort. If all else fails, be direct. Simply ask, "Honey, what can I do for you?"

While your wife's body language is more an indicator of how her day went, her appearance tells you how your wife is feeling about herself. How keen you are at observing this will go a long way in saying *I love you* to your wife.

Baggy sweats and old T-shirts are comfort wear, worn at very distinct times in your wife's life. This comfort ensemble is a sure sign your wife is feeling fat. Jeans, on the other hand, are contentment wear, worn when a woman is sure she will look good in them.

When a woman is feeling good about herself, she will take the time and effort to put on makeup and fix her hair. While I am not a big fan of either makeup or doing my hair, there is a distinct difference in both my hair and makeup on days when I am feeling good about myself as opposed to days when I am feeling not-so-good about myself. On a good day, I will run a brush through my hair and put on enough makeup to be presentable in public. If I decide to wear my hair up, I will take the time to make it look nice. However, on a not-so-good day, my hair will definitely be up—but a mess—and you won't see a trace of makeup.

I'll let you in on a secret. On the days I take special care to do my hair and makeup, I'm hoping Jay will notice and say something. Your wife cares more about what you think of how she looks than anyone else. Even when she is getting made-up for a special occasion, she is hoping *you* will be the one to compliment her. One wife said,

> I wish [my husband] made me feel valued and desired. Acting like [he] actually cared about my opinion or how I looked during daylight hours.

The surest way for your wife to take the time to fix her hair and put on makeup is for you to notice her good days and tell her how nice she looks!

How Does Your Wife Smell?

Last night, I (Jay) cooked hamburgers on the grill. There is no question that we are carnivores! We love our meat, and we particularly love it grilled over an open flame. The aroma emanating from the meat and spices caused neighbors to stop by wrapped in jealousy. As I brought the platter of burgers into the house, my family in unison said, "Ohhhhhh, that smells great!"

Just like aroma is intrinsically intertwined with the taste of food, the next two senses (smell and taste) are also intrinsically intertwined as they pertain to your wife. How she smells, i.e., her aroma, has to do with her emotional condition, while how she tastes is tied directly to her mental attitude.

I have read that animals can actually smell fear on a person. Further, when we run into someone who is very sure of themselves, we might say that person exudes confidence. We mean they give off an air or aroma of confidence.

Early in our ministry, Laura would speak maybe six to eight times a year. I could sense fear and anxiety in her as she stepped on the stage. Her emotional state was evident to me. Now, as we travel and speak virtually every weekend, Laura commands the stage from the moment she steps onto the platform. She is emotionally confident and controlled in situations that used to bring fear and anxiety.

In many marriages, emotional changes may not be as dramatic as in Laura's case. A husband who is keenly attuned to his wife's emotional state of being can quickly offer his support.

How Does Your Wife Taste?

Just as the aroma of the hamburger makes the mouth water, it is not until one takes a bite of the burger that the aroma gives way to the juicy, spicy grilled taste. Similarly a woman's emotional state eventually gives way to her mental attitude as it is fleshed out in her relationships.

Our Grace is affectionately called "Sweet-tart" by her papa (grandpa). He's chosen this nickname because he says she is either sweet or tart. He is right! There is no in between with her.

Grace has two very good friends at school. All three of these girls excel academically. They compete and push each other to get good grades. Sometimes, however, this competition can turn mean and ugly. The stress that Grace feels to compete with her friends turns our sweet cuddle bug Gracie into a screaming, crying, door-slamming nightmare. Her fear of failure in academics turns her mental attitude sour.

When you come home, ask a few quick questions to see how your wife smells and tastes.

Is your wife's greeting laced with sugar or vinegar?

Has the day left her with sweet memories or a bitter taste in her mouth?

Have the relationships she encountered during the day—
children, co-workers, friends—left her like fresh-baked pie
or curdled milk?

How Does Your Wife Feel?

At our Celebrate Your Marriage church workshops, we often
play the Newlywed Game as the after-lunch activity to get every-
body going again. The last question of the game is always for the
men. Here's the men's twenty-five-point bonus question: gentlemen, when your wife is feeling amorous, would you best describe
her as a playful puppy, cuddly kitten, or ferocious lion?

The counterquestion is: gentlemen, when your wife is irritated,
does she feel more like a piece of forty-grit sandpaper, a prickly
porcupine, or a cold ice princess? How does your wife respond
to your touch? Is she warm and cuddly or does she bristle when
you reach to touch her? I know if Jay has set me off in some way,
I can be that prickly porcupine when he touches me. Touch is a
sure way to sense the atmosphere around your home.

How Does Your Wife Sound?

The words your wife speaks, and the way in which she speaks
them, will be a clear indication of how she is feeling. I know for
myself, if I am not feeling good about myself, the words I speak
to my family are not kind ones—and are usually spoken in high-
decibel shrieks that make dogs run.

I am a screamer. I can admit it. When life has got me down,
I only stay quiet so long and then . . . boom! I explode. When I
start raising my voice or getting shrill in my tone, then my family
knows they had better tread lightly.

This is another area where women are very different. Some
wives are screamers like me. Other women respond in an opposite

fashion. Your wife may get quiet when she is upset or walking through self-esteem issues.

Rest assured this is not something Jay came into our marriage knowing about me! It may take some time to understand how your wife sounds in different situations and what her sounds are communicating.

Should I Stay or Can I Go?

Taking a few moments to assess how your wife looks, smells, feels, sounds, and tastes will give insight into the day she's had. In just a few short minutes you'll know whether you need to offer your help in the kitchen or if you can safely steal away to your recliner for a few unfettered minutes of relaxation.

Science Says

God made Eve from Adam's rib, but sometimes it seems like that's about all husbands and wives have in common. Science continually illuminates how very differently God created the two sexes. The following is an excerpt from *Brain Sex: The Real Difference Between Men and Women* by Anne Moir and David Jessel.

At a few hours old girls are more sensitive than boys to touch. Tests between the sexes of tactile sensitivity in the hands and fingers produce differences so striking that sometimes male and female scores do not even overlap, the most sensitive boy feeling less than the least sensitive girl. When it comes to sound, infant females are much less tolerant—one researcher believes that they may "hear" noises as being twice as loud as do males. Baby girls become irritated and anxious about noise, pain or discomfort more readily than baby boys.

Baby girls are more easily comforted by soothing words and singing. Even before they can understand language, girls seem to be better than boys at identifying the emotional content of speech. From the outset of life, girl babies show a greater interest in communicating with other people. One study involves babies of only 2–4 days old. It shows that girls spend almost twice as long maintaining eye contact with a silent adult, and girls also look longer than boys when the adult is talking. The boys' attention span was the same, whether the adult was talking or not—showing a relative bias towards what they could see, rather than what they could hear. From the cradle, baby girls like to gurgle at humans. Most boys are just as talkative, but are equally happy to jabber away at cot toys or looking at abstract geometric designs. Boys are more active and wakeful than girls—the male-wired brain of activity at work.

The female bias towards the personal shows itself in other ways. At four months, most baby girls can distinguish photographs of people they know from photographs of strangers; baby boys cannot.

The brain biases persist and strengthen as children grow up, "seeing" life through that particular filter of the brain which they find easier, and more natural, to use. That bias in girls towards the personal, for instance, shows up in experiments. A group of children was given a rather special sort of sight test. They looked through a contraption rather like a pair of binoculars, which showed the left and right eye two different images at the same time. One was of an object, the other of a person. The children had been shown exactly the same images, but when asked what they had seen gave different replies. Boys reported seeing significantly more things than people, and girls more people than things.[1]

Life experience bears out the findings of this scientific study: women are more acutely aware of the world around them than men. Following are some phrases I've commonly heard from Laura along with my responses.

Which do you prefer, eggshell or winter white?
Aren't they both white?

Did you hear that bumping noise?
No, I was asleep.

Ewwww, what's that smell?
Sorry, I forgot to brush my teeth.

These pillowcases feel rough.
My head doesn't care.

Ooooh, taste the tarragon in that stew?
Tarra what?

Guys, just like Laura's, your wives' senses are acute, which dictionary.com defines as keenly perceptive or discerning. On the other hand, your senses, just like mine, are dull as defined by dictionary.com as dense, imperceptive, obtuse, or moronic. So, what does all of this have to do with men actively showing our wives *I love you*? Simple—in addition to Five Sensing your wife when you come home from work, you also need to Five Sense yourself on a daily basis.

What Your Wife Sees

I love to wear T-shirts and sweatpants. If I'm not on the road traveling to an engagement—and sometimes even when I do travel—you will find me in the comfort of worn-out T-shirts and tattered sweats. I can go like this for days on end. I know that it's beginning to bother Laura when, as we get dressed in the morning, she states, "I'm thinking we should go out for lunch. I'm putting on slacks and a blouse. What are you wearing?" Laura is basically telling me, "Do you think you could care about the way you look for a change, for my sake?"

While the way your wife looks is important to you sexually, the way you keep yourself—your hair, beard, fingernails, and clothes—is an important way you can actively communicate *I love you* to your wife on a daily basis. Here is an example from a woman whose husband communicated very actively!

> That would be the time I was in labor with our first daughter. I had been in labor at this point for about 12½ hours. I was so uncomfortable and in so much pain. About three hours later, I was finally giving birth to our daughter and it seemed like it was taking forever. I remember my husband looking over at me with tears in his eyes and telling me "I love you" and what an awesome job I had done. Those words meant the world to me at that point. I could really *see* his love for me in his eyes.

What Your Wife Smells

I know I'm going to take some flack for what I'm about to say. I also know the 1,001 excuses men will give me. But here I go . . . Men, take a shower before you go to bed. Every night!

I don't understand how a man can jump into bed at night with the odor of a long day's work emanating from his pores and then expect his wife to be romantic. Quite frankly, I don't know how she can stand to lie beside him and sleep while he wallows in that grime for the next eight hours! Eck!

I am on a mission to get men to start taking their daily shower at night. Here are some of the excuses I hear and my simple replies:

A shower wakes me up in the morning.
So can drinking coffee, brushing your teeth, and cold water splashed in the face.

My skin gets too dry if I shower twice a day.
It's called lotion, dude, use it!

My hair is unmanageable unless I style it right out of the shower.
OK, Louise. If your hair is your priority in life, I guess I get that one.

I can't shave at night; I'll have five o'clock shadow.
So is it your boss you want kissing your cheek, or your wife?

I simply prefer my showers in the morning.
That's right, I forgot. Marriage is all about you and your preferences. Never mind we're talking about real-life ways to say I love you.

Seriously, how you smell means a ton to your wife. Remember, her sense of smell is much more acute. I can build a strong case that shows if you get into bed saying *I love you* to her sense of smell, she will say *I love you* in a way you clearly understand. This is where it pays to be a Boy Scout: always be prepared!

What Your Wife Feels

I love oxymorons—two words that simply don't seem to go together: jumbo shrimp, working vacation, virtual reality, silent scream, government organization, and my favorite, rap music. For years I thought the word *gentleman* was an oxymoron.

I am a rough guy. I break things. I am not subtle, quiet, or soft in any way—except around the midsection. My love taps on Laura's backside can leave red welts. My bear hugs actually make her feel like a bear is squeezing her last breath from her lungs.

Don't get me wrong, Laura is not a delicate rose petal of a woman. She will readily admit to being a tomboy growing up. She played college soccer at the highest levels, to the point of being invited to try out for the 1984 Women's Olympic Soccer Team. But the fact remains that she is still a woman who is very in tune to the way I touch her.

When I hold her hand while watching a movie, put my arm around her in church, or gently rub her back as she's making a salad, I actively tell her I love her. Some couples have come up with very creative ways to say *I love you*. Listen to this husband's creative way of communicating *I love you* to his wife, and at a time she needed to hear it more than ever.

All through our dating and married life we have had a little secret signal for I Love You. It's three squeezes of the hand or somewhere it can be felt on your person. Probably the most significant time I was able to communicate this to my wife was as she was being rolled into surgery prep for the removal of a lump in her breast. My simple three squeezes to her hand, with direct eye contact before she was rolled away on the gurney, was one of the most intimate moments of our marriage.

Some guys are slightly less creative . . . and less subtle. Take me, for instance. Early in our marriage, I took 1 Corinthians 7:4 literally:

The wife's body does not belong to her alone but also to her husband.

I would frequently reach for body parts that were once off limits. Laura would quickly retort, "Stop groping me!" The argument that I had a *right* to do this fell on deaf ears, and rightfully so. As I've matured, I've worked very hard to contain my groping reflex. I try diligently to touch Laura in very appropriate and loving ways. Maturity has also changed how I view this passage of Scripture. Laura's body is not mine alone, I share it with her.

Later she toned down her message a bit. Last summer the kids were both away at camp. Brilliant planning on our part, I must say. One evening during this week, after a particularly fun day together, we were making dinner. Laura was putting the finishing touches on our salad and I sidled up behind her and began to gently scratch her back. She turned to me and said, "Why don't you grope me anymore?" A bit dumbfounded I replied, "Because you told me you didn't like it." "Well," she admitted, "I was wrong." She had my attention, to say the least. "Mostly I don't like it, but there are times when it could be kind of fun." All I could think was yippee-ki-yay! You see, women love to be touched. Women love all kinds of touching. Most importantly, women love touching at the right time and in the right way.

What Your Wife Hears

I'm just a big kid at heart. That's probably why I went into youth ministry right out of college, trying to extend my youth in some subconscious way. As a youth minister, I took liberties with my bodily noises. Always up for a laugh or attention, I made sure that if gas was present, everyone was going to find out. Further, my sinuses have issues—big issues—resulting in my ability to snort, hack, and spew like a farmer. I was such a catch.

God blessed me with an understanding wife. Early in our marriage when I was performing amazing bodily noises for junior high students, or routinely engaging in my morning head-clearing ritual, Laura would simply utter the sarcastic word *pretty* and walk out of the room. I never realized what she was communicating.

In recent years Laura has plainly asked me, "Do you really *have* to do *that*?" I may not be the brightest bulb in the box, but I finally realized that my noises communicate something to her. At times, and I wish I could tell you exactly what times, my bodily noises really gross her out. When I'm mindful of my bodily noises and practice restraint, I communicate *I love you* to Laura.

Men, we can also communicate *I love you* by Five Sensing the way we speak to our wives. Earlier we discussed at length how tone of voice and inflection can speak more into a statement than just the words themselves. So we're not going to address that issue at length here, other than to remind you that your wife picks up heavily on your tone of voice. She also picks up on everyone else's tone of voice. Sometimes your wife needs you to step in and help when you sense that another's words are making her bristle. When we Five Sense how others speak to our wives, we have one more opportunity to communicate *I love you*.

Let me say right up front that our son, Torrey, is a great kid. He has, for the most part, been a joy to parent. He communicates well not only with his friends but also with adults. He even talks to us about issues on which many teens stay mute. That being said, he is still a teenager.

From time to time (okay, more and more these days) Torrey will be out at night. He'll be off to a ball game, Campus Life meeting, or youth group activity. While he's gone, we get Grace to bed and actually have some quality time as a couple: sometimes talking, sometimes reading, sometimes sitting in front of the TV. Often we will start to connect in a way that would naturally lead to additional connecting in the bedroom.

Enter Torrey. We try to engage him in conversation about his evening's activities. More often than not, he can't wait to spill the plot lines that unfolded over his night out. However, from time to time—like when he's tired, irritated at a friend, or just not in the mood to talk—he refuses to communicate about his night. I usually dismiss it. As a man I understand when another guy just doesn't feel like talking. But Laura can get pretty bent out of shape.

His refusal to communicate can really set her off. Laura's sensitivity to our son's attitude is transferred to her attitude. Without even realizing what's happening, all of our earlier connecting suddenly vanishes, along with my hopes for further connection.

When I step in and say, "Torrey, your mom is asking you questions that are important to her. Please show her some respect and answer them," I actively show Laura that I love her by being sensitive to her sensitivities. I have Five Sensed my wife's irritation at our son and the fact that it will have an impact on her mood. When I help diffuse the situation, she sees that I understand her and I am actively saying *I love you*.

What Your Wife Tastes

I don't know anyone who doesn't like a good kiss. For a woman, however, this can be one of the most intimate acts on the planet. We don't typically give illustrations from R-rated movies, but this one speaks volumes.

Do you remember the movie *Pretty Woman*, starring Julia Roberts and Richard Gere? Roberts's character was a hooker.

She lived her life and paid her bills by allowing men to have sex with her. During their first sexual encounter, Roberts tells Gere that he can do anything he wants for the right price, except—you guessed it—kiss her. Kissing is off limits—the one sexual activity too intimate even for a woman who sells her body for sex.

When a man takes the time to Five Sense how he tastes to his wife before kissing her, he communicates loudly *I love you*. Bitter coffee, stale beer, overpowering garlic, and smoker's ashtray breath are all quick ways to turn *I love you* into *yuck*.

We have a friend who likes a good cigar from time to time. The aroma, the taste, and the long draw on the smoldering stick relax him after a tiring day at work. His wife had made her position clear: on nights he says yes to a cigar, he also says no to her. Brushing his teeth, using mouthwash, and eating a host of breath mints cannot prevent the rancid taste he leaves in her mouth when he kisses her good night. A simple choice, but a profound truth: she can't stand the way his kiss tastes after an evening spent sucking on a stogie. Therefore, if he is planning on connecting physically with his wife on any given evening, he should Five Sense the way he tastes and choose not to smoke that cigar!

For you and your wife, it may not be a cigar. It may be coffee, garlic, or beer. As husbands who care, we all need to be sensitive to what our kiss tastes like to our wives. Often, Laura and I will mutually agree not to put those onions on our dinner salad for this very reason.

Love Is in the Air

Men, *I love you* is a powerful phrase wives need to hear from you every day. Fortunately, you have an opportunity to communicate this powerful phrase with more than mere words. Doing so will cause your bride to be giddy, intoxicated, and head over heels in love with you. When you Five Sense not only your wife but also yourself, you'll enhance the environment in your home and create an atmosphere that continually communicates *I love you* to your wife.

Questions for Reflection

- Questions for her:
  - Is this an important phrase for you? Why or why not?
  - When your husband communicates *I love you*, how do you respond?
  - What is the most powerful way he communicates *I love you*?
  - Identify a particular point or story from this chapter that may help your spouse understand this need better.
  - As we walk through these different phrases it will become apparent that you have one or two that you need to hear more than the others. Keep a tally as to the priority level you believe each one takes in your life.
  - Rank in order of priority (one through four, one being the highest priority):
    - I love you
    - I respect you
    - I desire you
    - I cherish you
- Questions for him:
  - Do you feel you communicate this phrase frequently enough for your wife? Why or why not?

- Do you think you communicate *I love you* in ways she understands?
- Identify an "aha" moment in this chapter that reinforced your understanding of this need in the life of your spouse.
- What did you think about the Five Sensing section? Have you ever thought of Five Sensing your wife or yourself?

3

He Needs to Hear "I'm Proud of You"

I am so proud my Jay is in big-boy underwear.

Jay's mom after potty training him, 1963

Every man is searching for significance. Granted, sometimes we look in the wrong places. No matter where a man looks, very little compares to knowing that the woman he loves—the woman he wants to spend the rest of his life with—is proud of him. I'm not necessarily talking about being proud of what he does for a living, his education, or his good looks—though those don't hurt. But wives, if you want to see your man walk taller, tell him you are proud of him for what really matters in life:

- I'm proud of the way you play with the children.
- I'm proud of the way you help out around the house.
- I'm proud of the way you take care of the cars so I don't have to do a thing with them.

We work with countless couples in crisis. Most of the time we will start a session by asking some simple, yet revealing, questions. First we ask the husband, "What is it about your wife that you love? What about her is special?" He can just rattle off the compliments. It usually doesn't matter how upset he is or how heated their relationship has been, the husband can come up with many attributes he finds appealing about his wife.

We often get the opposite response when we turn to the wife and ask, "What is it about your husband that you're proud of?" Often she's at a loss. Nothing. Nada. We watch her husband wither before our eyes. That is the power—the significance—of this phrase, or the lack of it. Hearing, or not hearing, those words can make or break any man.

Mike and Mara

On the outside, Mike and Mara looked like most typical married couples. Living in a modest house with all the comforts of middle class America, they had four beautiful kids who were involved in many school and church activities. Mike was a teacher who took extra jobs in the summer to make ends meet while Mara stayed at home caring for the many needs of their children.

We first met with this couple because "things were not right in their relationship." Mara felt Mike was distancing himself from her, pouring more and more of himself into his work, their kids, and the church. He seemed to be giving himself to every aspect of his life—except his marriage. As we began to talk through the issues of their marriage, it became increasingly clear that Mara was a woman who was never satisfied.

No matter what Mike did—how much money he made, how much time he devoted to the kids, or how much time he spent helping at church—Mara could not say anything positive about Mike or his contribution to their marriage and family. It was as if Mara measured Mike's every move by her preconceived image of the "perfect husband." Whenever Mike didn't fit that image, she was going to let him know. To make matters worse, Mara was all too happy to share her husband's substandard performance with anyone who would listen.

Mike felt humiliated, lacked confidence, and in general considered himself a failure. He confided that they hadn't had sexual relations since Mara became pregnant with their fourth child. His candid comment spoke volumes. "I'm not sure I'd want to." Mike had resigned himself to a life of both private and public ridicule. "I wish just once she would tell me I did something right, then I would know that I pleased her."

Why It's So Important to Us

No one can deny the connection between a mother and her newborn baby. For nine months the two are inextricably connected. In the months following birth, a connection continues that a father will never know. This bond from birth sets the stage for the significant role a mother's approval, and subsequently a wife's approval, plays in a man's life.

For some of you this is going to sound silly, and maybe it is, but a man's earliest memories of Mom have to do with hearing the words "I'm so proud of you!" From baby's first steps to potty training to the first day of school, you can see a child's chest puff out when Mommy says, "I'm so proud of you." It's hardwired into our psyche.

Dictionary.com defines *encourage* as "to inspire with courage." When you tell your husband you are proud of him, you inspire him with courage. He may gain the courage to play thirty minutes longer with the kids. He may be emboldened to tackle that entire "honey do" list. Whatever he is doing, when he hears those words from you, he will be challenged, inspired, and motivated to tackle even more the next time.

The Power of Seeing Results

My dad was a youth minister all his adult life. He began his career with Youth for Christ the same year I was born and faithfully ministered for over forty years. He served in many local communities as well as on a national level with this wonderful youth evangelism organization.

He served in Petoskey, Michigan, from 1969 until 1984. During the oil embargo of the early 1970s, my dad decided we needed to heat our home with a woodstove. The cast-iron woodstove would radiate heat throughout our house in the dead of winter at a fraction of the cost of heating oil or natural gas. The only catch? We had to cut the wood ourselves.

And so began our family's routine of cutting and stacking firewood. OK, let's be honest: Dad and I cut and stacked. Mom and Diane got a free pass. During late summer and early fall, our Saturdays and weekday afternoons were spent in the woods felling trees. We cut, split, and stacked cord upon cord of hardwood to heat our home during the winter. For me it was nothing but back-breaking work. For my dad it was a labor of love.

Cutting wood was like a hobby for my dad. He spent time scouting dead trees, took his chain saw to be sharpened and tuned up. He even bought special clothing and boots. He was like a deer hunter getting buck fever. I couldn't figure out his love for cutting wood.

One beautiful September Saturday, during my junior year in high school, we were out cutting an incredible oak. The hardwood of that oak tree burned hot and long. With just that one tree, we could heat our home nearly all winter through. Dad was giddy with excitement over his find.

I took that opportunity to satisfy my curiosity. "Dad, why do you have such a love for felling, cutting, and stacking wood?" He replied, "Son, life in the ministry rarely affords quantifiable results. I spend a lot of time with people: helping people, praying with people, praying for people, serving people. At the end of the day, I never really know if my efforts helped. The end result is God's department. I often wonder if my work has accomplished anything."

He continued. "Cutting wood offers immediate feedback. At the end of the day I can see that we've cut and stacked three, four, five cords of wood. Seeing those quantifiable results, knowing I have accomplished something in my life, gives me great satisfaction. My self-worth doesn't depend on whether or not I cut the wood, but cutting the wood does give me a sense of pride in a job I can see."

All men share this need to see the fruit of their labors. Men are goal oriented. It may not be a professional goal. Your husband's goals might have to do with a hobby or project around the house. For your husband it may be that classic car he just restored or that deer he just harvested. It doesn't flesh out the same way for every man. Whatever the goal is, when he achieves it, acknowledge the accomplishment (like Cheryl does below).

My husband has been a stay at home father for six and a half years. It's difficult for him to be out of the workforce and have a wife who is solely in the "provider" role. During the past six years, Charles attended community college (a big step for someone who did not do well in high school). This past May, Charles graduated with two associate degrees, with honors and as a member of Phi Theta Kappa honor society. I communicated verbally and nonverbally how proud I was that he set and reached his goal.

Cheryl

When you become aware of what brings your husband that sense of accomplishment and you acknowledge it, you will speak volumes to him about how much you care.

This Preacher Is a Golfer

My passion for the game of golf is no secret. One of the reasons I love golf is that it provides instant quantifiable feedback. Every shot is an opportunity to accomplish your goal: a good drive that lands in the fairway, a laser-like iron shot that never leaves the pin, and the unmistakable sound of a birdie putt hitting the bottom of the cup. For me, pride of accomplishment comes in the form of a respectable golf score. When Laura acknowledges my accomplishment, she lets me know she is proud of me.

As with my father and wood, this is not a defining aspect of who I am, but it is a measurable part of my life. Golf gives me a sense of accomplishment. Laura's recognition of my accomplishment gives me a sense of significance. For your husband, it may not be cutting wood or playing golf, but there is something that gives him a sense of accomplishment.

Overcoming Mind-sets

One thing you will never read in our books is that we have these ideas mastered. Our marriage, just like every other, is a work in progress. Even after twenty-four years of marriage, I have to backtrack and apologize for not telling Jay how proud I am of him.

In order to give our husbands the admiration they need, we may need to overcome some predisposed mind-sets. In surveying and speaking to hundreds of women, Jay and I know that each wife struggles with overcoming different mind-sets. Identifying your personal battle is the first step to gaining the freedom to affirm your husband's accomplishments, so he doesn't have to look in unhealthy places for his significance as a man.

Mind-set #1: I'm Not Going to Feed His Ego

I jokingly tell audiences that a sharp tongue is my spiritual gift. No, I'm not being sacrilegious; I'm actually confessing a problem that plagued our marriage for years. Sharp-tongue-ness is a defense mechanism that I grew up with and brought into our marriage. We were married for over ten years before Jay ever heard me say the words *I'm proud of you.*

Jay's mom always encouraged him and told him he could accomplish anything he set his mind to. When he was a young man, she always told him how proud she was of him. Her encouragement imbued Jay with a sense of confidence.

The self-confidence and self-assurance that first attracted me to Jay began to come across as ego. I became convinced it was my mission in life to make sure he didn't get too big for his britches. While I didn't necessarily cut Jay down, especially in public, I also never edified him. Whenever he'd come home and share some accomplishment, my response was simply a calm, cool, "That's nice."

My perspective was challenged when I read a story about Ruth Bell Graham, wife of preacher Billy Graham. Ruth shared a revelation she had about her role in Billy's life. For a long time she thought it was her duty to keep Billy humble and make him good. At a pivotal point in their relationship, she realized that keeping Billy humble and making him good were supernatural acts that could only be accomplished by God himself. Ruth came to a new understanding of her role as a wife: "My job is to love and encourage him in everything he does."

Suddenly I realized I had read my job description wrong. My job wasn't to passively or aggressively keep Jay humble. That's God's job. God knows far better than me when Jay is getting too big for his britches, and even better how to keep him humble. My job is to make sure that Jay knows I'm proud of him—proud of Jay the father, Jay the husband, and Jay the man.

Mind-set #2: What's the Big Deal?

Jay and I had planned a golf getaway weekend with our good friends Russ and Joneen Wight. We had blocked off our schedule, Grandma was on kid duty, and our minds were clear to have fun!

Our two-hour ride from Alma was filled with laughter and anticipation. We arrived at the Black Bear golf course in Vanderbilt, Michigan, at 10:15 a.m. The boys had ample time to hit some warm-up balls and get in a few practice putts while the girls checked out the deals in the pro shop before our 11:00 a.m. tee time.

I enjoy golfing, but Jay is the real fan of the game. An avid golfer, he usually shoots in the mid-seventies. But this particular summer he couldn't find his swing. Prior to our weekend at Black Bear, his best score had been an eighty-two. But this day he was feeling it. He finished the front nine at thirty-six, even par. His best round of the summer was clearly in sight.

Somewhere around hole thirteen, Joneen and I checked out. One of us said something that made the other start to giggle, and the remaining five holes turned into a giggle fest. We were still swinging our clubs, but our focus wasn't on the game. We couldn't hit the ball half the time and could no longer remember our score. Why? Because we were having too much fun to care! Jay was shooting his best game of the summer with a good friend by his side, and Joneen and I were enjoying our girl time. It should have been the perfect afternoon, but something didn't feel right.

When we returned home, Jay confided, "I shot a seventy-eight—by far the best round of the summer—but it felt empty because I couldn't share it with you." While Jay was enjoying his time with Russ, he missed having his wife acknowledge his accomplishment. Every giggle I shared with Joneen was like me telling Jay, "I don't care that you are shooting the best round of your summer." Without saying a word, I had communicated, "I'm not proud of what you are doing. I'm not proud of you."

Like I said, I enjoy golf, but it's just a game. I enjoy golfing well, and I do get upset if I shoot poorly. However, a year from now, I won't be able to tell you what I scored on any given course. Not so with Jay. Jay gets a great sense of accomplishment from golfing well. I know that, but still I failed to recognize the importance of that day for him. I was too wrapped up in what was immediately important to me (having fun with a girlfriend) to share in his success.

What's your husband into? His work? Fishing? A side project? Whatever it is, you might not really get it. You might not understand why he thinks it's the best thing ever. But if you can recognize what brings him a sense of accomplishment and express your appreciation for his achievement—that he performed well—you will be giving him a precious gift: significance in the eyes of his beloved.

Mind-set #3: He Does Nothing to Make Me Proud

In *The Birth Order Book* Dr. Kevin Leman describes different personality traits that arise as a result of where you fall in relation to your siblings. For example, when a firstborn woman (type A personality) marries a middle or last-born man (carefree personality), she often interprets his personality as unmotivated, unproductive, or downright lazy. Here's the story of a lovely lady (Michelle) who was bringing up one very lazy husband (Bob).

Maybe you know someone like Bob. The first thing you notice about him is his infectious, disarming smile. The baby of his family, Bob has a hearty handshake and a belly laugh that endear him to virtually everyone.

Bob has more God-given talent in his little finger than most of us possess in our entire bodies. Bob grasps new concepts quickly, is a creative brainstormer, and is a self-taught computer prodigy. But to Bob's wife, Michelle, all of his talent, all of his charm, and all of his personality seemed to be a waste as Bob flitted from one job to another, from one scheme to the next. Bob's job instability continually left his family economically challenged. Michelle had spent so much time focused on their lack that she had to rack her brain to find any reason to be proud of Bob.

Michelle's breakthrough came when Jay asked her this simple question: "Why did you marry Bob in the first place?" Michelle replied, "He is so much fun!" Jay challenged her perspective. "Then be proud of Bob for his ability to see the brighter side of life even in tough times." That one comment turned the tide. Michelle continued, "He is such a good friend. He never turns down someone in need." Jay suggested, "Then be proud of his character." Michelle's eyes sparkled as she said, "He is such a good dad." Jay encouraged her, "Then tell him you are proud that your children will grow up in a loving family."

As Michelle found out, with a little bit of effort you can find areas of your husband's life that make you proud of him.

Mind-set #4: He Does Not Deserve My Admiration

Maybe your mind-set has been crushed by infidelity. Your husband has been unfaithful to the commitment of your marriage. A husband's sexual infidelity, financial irresponsibility, and addictions all leave a woman feeling betrayed and vulnerable. That pain fosters a mind-set that says he does not deserve admiration. You may withhold admiration as a punishment for what he has done.

As you begin to operate out of a place of mistrust, withholding admiration feels like a way to protect your heart.

As obvious as your husband's sin may be, this mind-set reveals your sin: unforgiveness. While hurt and pain may be immense, the only way out of the pain is to forgive. "Therefore confess your sins to each other and pray for each other so that you may be healed" (James 5:16).

When you forgive, you are trusting God with your heart. You trust him to deal with the offenses that have been committed against you. Just as it is God's responsibility to keep your husband humble, it is also God's responsibility to convict your husband of his sin. Nothing, absolutely nothing, in me can bring about that change in my husband. No amount of crying, no amount of pouting, no amount of sex withholding. There is not a cold shoulder icy enough to freeze your husband into repentance. Unforgiveness, in its many forms, will only harden your heart and make you more unlovely.

While repentance is your husband's responsibility, forgiveness is yours. Romans 5:8: "But God demonstrates his own love for us in this: While we were still sinners, Christ died for us." The example is clear; we were forgiven before we repented.

The healing power of God's forgiveness clears your mind of the wrong that has been done and releases you from the pain so you can *see* the qualities in your husband that deserve your admiration. Forgiveness softens your heart so you can once again *feel* admiration for your husband.

Just Say It

As you overcome these mind-sets you will begin to feel admiration for your husband. Hopefully, you've identified at least one area of your husband's life, character, or talents that you are proud of. But saying it? Well, that just feels weird. Many women are just as uncomfortable saying, "I'm proud of you," as men are uneasy saying, "I love you."

Perhaps, like this husband, you said it early on in your relationship, when love was new and made you do and say amazing things.

> Right after we were engaged I had to work a twenty-six-hour shift. She came to my work when I was done, made sure I made it home safely, and then proceeded to clean my apartment . . . leaving a note saying how proud she was going to be to be my wife.

What if the last time your husband said "I love you" was on your wedding day? Would you still be feeling that love today? In the same way you need to regularly hear *I love you*, your husband needs to hear *I'm proud of you* repeated throughout your marriage.

A husband can hear *I'm proud of you* from a boss, co-worker, or friend, but when he hears it from his wife, it touches his heart and deepens his commitment to the relationship. Here are just two responses from our survey:

> A couple of weeks ago, Allison said to me, "You are a remarkable man." Well, here it is two weeks later, and I am still basking in it.

> I found a note in my car one morning. It was from my wife and told me how proud she was of me. I bawled for ten minutes. I think it was the first time she'd ever said that in fourteen years of marriage. It meant a lot and still does.

Understand the power of that gesture. He bawled for ten minutes and he still remembers the occasion to this day. That was a defining moment in his marriage, and rest assured it gave him a renewed love and affection for his wife.

When you utter the words *I'm proud of you*, you will see your man stand up straighter and focus more clearly. That's a response worth overcoming whatever uneasiness you may feel. The more you say it, the easier it gets. So, just say it!

Say It in Crisis

Saying *I'm proud of you* during times of crisis is particularly powerful.

During the Sept 11, 2001, crisis, my husband was the one who did the transponder translations for the flights that crashed. His expertise and communication skills were very important for our nation. Knowing the incredible stress of this job and the way he handled it made me extremely proud and honored.

I love movies with happy endings. I especially enjoy movies when, despite adversity, the guy ends up with the girl on his arm. This survey respondent gave that happy ending feeling to her husband. In the midst of that unthinkable tragedy, she acknowledged her husband's heroic contribution to our nation. The sense of significance she gave her husband that day forever changed the meaning of 9/11 for one man. How will your husband remember your response in times of crisis?

Say It in Front of Your Family

Saying *I'm proud of you* is especially important when it comes to dealing with family.

Just today I told him I was proud of him because he actually picked up the phone and reconnected with his father, who he hasn't spoken to in about four years. It opened the door for them to reconnect, then he took the ball and ran through that door. He normally wouldn't have done that, so I felt very happy for him and his dad. It was a challenge for him, and he met that challenge head on.

We had dinner with family members who are not believers. They asked many questions and sometimes became hostile with their words. Norm held firm and stood firmly on God's Word. In love he was able to communicate the Truth and Love found in God's Word. Even though they did not accept what we said as their Truth, seeds had been planted. After we said good night to my family and were walking to our car, I told him I was proud of him, and that I loved him and his passion for the Lord more than ever.

Telling your husband you are proud of how he interacts with family is important. Speaking all of these phrases in front of others is also essential. When we speak these phrases in front of family, we begin to establish our own identity as a couple, as well as boundaries for other relationships.

Say It in Front of Your Kids

Because *I'm proud of you* and *I believe in you* are crucial to the development of our husbands as leaders in our homes, we need to speak these words in front of our kids!

When we started a family, we purchased a Red Plate, which is an actual red plate that is used to celebrate special occasions. We used it for birthdays and first "this or that" for the kids. One day, I pulled it out and served my husband's dinner on it. We celebrated him as a husband and father. We told him how proud we are of him and how thankful we are for all he does for us.

It is no secret that many kids in our culture are missing positive male role models. Saying the phrase *I'm proud of you* to your husband—in front of your kids—helps your children understand what it means to be a man. This is a necessary step in nurturing your sons to become authentic men and in helping your daughters identify authentic men when choosing a spouse.

If at First You Don't Succeed

I (Jay) like to journal . . . I started journaling when I was seventeen years old, just out of high school, and traveling full time with a Christian rock band. OK, rock band maybe isn't the best way to describe our music, which sounded more like Chicago than the Rolling Stones, but you get the point. I thought it would be a great way to document my thoughts, feelings, and revelations I would have during my first year "on my own."

Over the years my journaling has taken on many forms, and now I even keep a prayer journal. I enjoy writing my thoughts about the Lord and about the way he moves in my life and putting my requests to him in black and white. From time to time those prayers come out as a poem. I'm no Robert Frost, but my poems mean a lot to me, and I believe they mean a lot to the Lord; in fact, I think he's particularly fond of them. At first blush, most are pretty elementary and at times a little sappy, but hey, they are mine . . . deal with it!

One particular week Laura and I were trying to find a creative way to inspire parents, and dads in particular, to reflect on being a parent. I suggested we send out the following poem, not telling Laura it was one of mine.

A Father's Reflection

From starry skies to foaming seas
I see the signs—your love for me.

A baby's laugh, a good friend's grin
Your love displayed, it pulls me in.

A wretched man, my sin, my shame
I'm only cleansed by Jesus' Name.

His name alone can calm the sea
His blood the Cross has set me free.

I'm thankful for my wife and kids
And also for what Jesus did.

Lord hear my prayer, that is my plea
What is the life you have for me?

When I asked her what she thought, her reply was "It's OK
. . . a little on the sappy side, but it might work." At that point I
said, "Well, I know I'm no Longfellow, but I did write it from my
heart." Her mouth dropped open and her eyes bugged out. "*You*
wrote that? I thought you pulled it off some Internet site. I can't
believe you wrote that, it's amazing, you're so sensitive, you're so
deep, I'm so proud of you!" Yes, she missed it the first time, but
her words still meant a lot when she did say them.

A "Zinger" of a Time

The year 2008 was proving to be a pivotal year for the American
Ryder Cup golf team. After almost a decade of dominance by the
Europeans, Captain Paul Azinger was charged with winning the
Ryder Cup and bringing it back to American soil. Zinger, as he
is known in golf circles, was up to the task.

Nick Faldo, captain of the 2008 European team, and Zinger
had a long history. Their rivalry dated back to the 1987 Brit-

ish Open at Murfield Golf Club. Zinger bogeyed the last two holes, placing him in a tie for second place. Meanwhile, Faldo made par on all eighteen holes, securing his first win in a Major golf tournament. Zinger would eventually win a Major; Faldo won six.

With a 2–0–2 record, Zinger led Faldo in Ryder Cup head-to-head matches; however, Faldo holds the record for most Ryder Cup appearances and total points won in a career. The rivalry has deepened in recent years as the two have moved from on-course competitors to television commentators. Zinger plays the stoic, straight man to Faldo's suave, comedic style.

In an interview with *Golf Digest* Zinger confessed, "Yeah, I've felt my accomplishments have been minimized in comparison with Nick's. I try to brush it off, brush it off, but that's the real feeling. There is always a little something there."

Your husband may not be faced with an internationally televised sporting event, but his challenges are equally weighty in his world. He may be dealing with a boss who's unfair, poor working conditions, or a job he finds unsatisfying. The reality of life for men is that our feelings are tied to our accomplishments. When you—the most important person in your husband's life—acknowledge your husband's accomplishments, you inspire him to become the man of your dreams.

By the way, the U.S. team, captained by Azinger, dominated the Europeans 16½ to 11½.

Questions for Reflection

- Questions for him:
  - Is this an important phrase for you? Why or why not?

- When your wife communicates *I am proud of you*, how do you respond?
- What is the most powerful way she communicates *I am proud of you*?
- Identify a particular point or story from this chapter that may help your spouse understand this need better.
- As we walk through these different phrases, it will become apparent that you have one or two that you need to hear more than the others. Keep a tally as to the priority level you believe each one takes in your life.
- Rank in order of priority (one through four, one being the highest priority):
  - I am proud of you
  - I need (*blank*) from you
  - I want you
  - I believe in you
- Questions for her:
  - Do you feel you communicate this phrase frequently enough for your husband? Why or why not?
  - Do you think you communicate "I am proud of you" in ways he understands?
  - Identify an "aha" moment in this chapter that reinforced your understanding of this need in the life of your spouse.
  - What did you think about the "mind-sets" section? Have you ever thought you had an improper mind-set regarding being proud of your husband?

4

She Needs to Hear "I Respect You"

Her children respect and bless her;
    her husband joins in with words of praise:
"Many women have done wonderful things,
    but you've outclassed them all!"
Charm can mislead and beauty soon fades.
    The woman to be admired and praised
    is the woman who lives in the Fear-of-GOD.
Give her everything she deserves!
    Festoon her life with praises!

Proverbs 31:28–31 The Message

W e begin the other "She Needs to Hear" chapters with Laura explaining to men why women need to hear a particular phrase. But I (Jay) am going to start this chapter off. Historically, the church has instructed women to respect their husbands, and we agree this is fundamental to a healthy marriage. However, men aren't the only ones who need to be respected.

Love and Respect

Laura and I joke that in our relationship I am often more of a girl than she is. Unfair stereotypes aside, I am the one who loves to hold hands and cuddle. I am much more sensitive to harsh words, and I actually care if my clothes are ironed.

What's even more interesting is that I need and want love more than I need or want respect. Laura is the one in our relationship who needs and wants respect more so than love. Some might say it's the way we were brought up or that we're genetic freaks of nature. We simply believe that men and women *both* need love and respect. Further, these needs are not mutually exclusive of each other.

R-E-S-P-E-C-T—Tell You What It Means to Me

"She is your mother and you will respect her on this issue" is an often repeated refrain in our home. I tell our teenage son this for two reasons. One, as a growing man he needs to learn to respect women. Two, I know how much it means to Laura.

So, what is this thing called respect, and why do women need it?

Respect is defined as:

To hold in esteem or honor.

To show regard or consideration.

Every human needs respect. As we walk through the self-esteem issues of adolescence and mature into adulthood, respect—or a lack of respect—molds our psyche. Scripture, in addition to life experience, emphasizes the need for every person to give and receive respect.

Be devoted to one another in brotherly love. Honor one another above yourselves.

Romans 12:10

Do nothing from selfishness or empty conceit, but with humility of mind regard one another as more important than yourselves.

Philippians 2:3 NASB

Show proper respect to everyone: Love the brotherhood of believers, fear God, honor the king.

1 Peter 2:17

Survey Says

Not surprisingly, our survey results support Scripture.

After a particularly difficult day for her, mostly because of the chaos that is parenthood, I told her how proud I was of the mom she is.

What a terrific job she's done raising her kids (my stepkids) pretty much by herself for the first seven to eleven years of their lives.

Being involved in ministry, I do a lot of "big" programs for the children at our church. No matter how many comments I receive from other people, it means so much when I hear him say that it went well. And to hear him talk about it to other people means even more.

My husband communicates respect when we are in the presence of others and he says things like, "She's really good at that." He thinks that I have more gifts and abilities than I think that I have!

Superwoman

Society tells a woman that in order to gain respect, she must be Superwoman. She must have a full-time job outside of the home, she must be Supermom, and she must be Superwife. She must love her husband and give him sex every day. If she falls short in any of these areas, she is less than a complete woman. This drive to be Superwoman, in an attempt to earn respect, is leading to some devastating results.

Here is an excerpt from an article in *Advocate Health Centers* magazine, published in 2003.

For many American women, rushing from work to home to school—then getting up and doing it all over again—has become the norm. Juggling a spouse, children, boss and friends all adds up to a hectic lifestyle that can put your physical and mental health in the dumps.
Women and stress
According to some experts, the stress and anxiety that busy career women live with brings more than the occasional stressful

day that can be mellowed with a quiet night with hubby or happy hour with the girls—it can lead to a medical condition that's been dubbed "hurried woman syndrome."

"Symptoms include fatigue, moodiness, weight gain and low sex drive," says Chandrarekha Kaza, MD, an internist at the Advocate Health Center—Palos Heights. "And approximately 50 million American women have at least one of these symptoms."

The illness is thought to be triggered by chronic stress and poor lifestyle choices, and its main victims are women ages 25 to 55. Though the jury is still out among the medical community as to whether hurried woman syndrome is a true illness, there's no disagreement that the stress and tension endured by women can lead to very real health problems.

Women are more vulnerable than men to stress-induced illnesses for a variety of reasons, reports the American Medical Women's Association. "Women are still the natural caregivers in families," Dr. Kaza explains. "In many households, women commonly come home after working a full day only to continue working—there are meals to be cooked and children to be tended to."

I (Laura) know that in my own life, I had to come to a point where I had to learn to say no to activities that were all well and good but were skewing my priorities. My inability to say no to being on every church and school committee began to cause stress in my life and marriage. While some may think this is just a North American phenomenon, in actuality this "Hurried Woman Syndrome" (HWS) is being felt worldwide. Take this information published on Boloji.com by Kavita Devgan, June 5, 2005.

In India, urban women have to tackle similar pressures of home, office and other responsibilities. "High stress and anxiety levels, mild depression, physical exhaustion, digestive disorders, low sex drive, unnatural weight gain and low self-esteem are all indicators that something is not right," says Dr. Manju Mehta, Professor of Clinical Psychiatry, AIIMS, while explaining how to detect HWS.

The root cause of HWS is chronic stress. "There are many kinds of stress and they vary from person to person. Sometimes, stress can't be avoided. However, in the case of a majority of the women, most of the stress can be avoided or managed better. These avoidable stresses are those that often come from a busy, hectic schedule and lifestyle choices that people make," says Dr. Avdesh Sharma, Director of Parivartan Center for Mental Health, Hauz Khas, New Delhi.

Dr. Sharma says that women are so adept at multi-tasking that they keep doing it without even realizing the damage it is causing them. "Stop being a superwoman," he tells his patients.

An article by Robin Yapp, published in the *London Daily Mail* on April 30, 2005, speaks of the impact HWS has in European homes. The serious health problems accompanying HWS should give pause to any woman and cause her to look at her lifestyle and the choices she is making.

Now the British Osteopathic Association has warned that more than three-quarters of women suffer from at least one chronic health problem, compared with 48 percent of men.

Nigel Graham, BOA president, said: "It's occurring a lot, particularly with women in London who have high-pressure jobs and who may have a young family and are trying to do everything at once—running off to the gym at lunch time and then doing the shopping before going home."

Earlier this year a survey of 10,000 British women by *Prima* magazine found three-quarters had at least five symptoms of HWS. It warned that the combination of symptoms can often be a precursor to clinical depression or a more serious illness.

I began to reduce the stress of a hectic and overcommitted schedule when Jay and I developed our family mission statement. The mission statement gave me power to say yes to those commitments that furthered our mission and freedom to say no to those requests that came along that detracted from our mission statement.

As a result of prioritizing my commitments through the filter of a family mission statement, I became a healthier woman, wife, and mother. Women are trying to be everything to everyone and they simply can't. On every continent, science is showing they can't. Superwoman has left the building.

A Brief History Lesson

So how did our society get to the point of putting women in the position of needing to be just like men? Let's take a brief look at history.

For centuries in America, husband and wife worked together side by side. Farm work was done by both sexes, and family businesses were staffed by both spouses.

With the onset of the industrial revolution, men left the farm and headed to the factory in order to earn a steady paycheck. The factory offered security not provided by the farming life. As men began to work outside of the home, division of labor inside the home became a reality. Men's work and women's work were born.

World War II took many men from the workforce. Out of necessity, factories opened their doors to women. "Rosie the Riveter" soon realized that she could do the very job once thought reserved for a man. That job was a source of increased income, resulting in a higher standard of living for "Rosie" and her family.

Unlike the man who went to the factory and returned home to a wife who had spent the day cleaning and cooking, "Rosie" returned to an unkempt home with no meal waiting. Once home from the factory, "Rosie" still had a day's work ahead of her—cooking, cleaning, and doing laundry. Somewhere along the way, society said women had to do it all to be valuable. We fell for the lie that we have to prove we are just as good as or better than men. Guys, I don't want to be just like you. That's not a cut on you. I simply want to be who God created me to be. Deep down inside, so does your wife.

It seems to us that our society is pushing women to be more like men. However, Scripture tells us that men and women were created different, still in the image of God, but different. We as women are trying to figure out how the two mesh together. So in the midst of this cultural pressure, your wife needs to hear *I respect you.* You can tell her that by encouraging her in her gifts and abilities. You see them, you know what they are. You know what your wife is passionate about and what she is gifted to do. She needs to hear that you believe in her gifts and that you understand her passion.

You could say it this way:

Honey, I recognize the Lord has gifted you to do (*blank*), and the Lord has given you a passion to do it so . . . go for it!

Your wife may pursue a full-time career. She may want to be an accountant because she is gifted with numbers. She may want to be a psychologist because she understands people. She may want to be a schoolteacher because she is passionate about kids. Encourage her in those dreams. If the Lord has gifted her to stay home with your children, affirm for her how important you think her calling is. Whatever your wife's dream, when you tell her *I respect you*, she is a free woman! She is free to be capable, accomplished, and significant.

Free Her to Be Capable

Every wife wants to know her husband supports her dreams—whether pursuing a hobby, furthering her career, or choosing to be a stay-at-home mother. If you were to ask your wife what she has always wanted to do—but has not yet done—what would she say? Do you know? If not, ask her. Then give her permission to do it! I use that word *permission* in the sense that you are giving her the encouragement she needs to step out and make her dreams a reality. This woman's husband gets it right.

> Just over four years ago, I was working a full-time job at the local bank and raising two girls and a third one on the way. I was really having a hard time with the fact that my babysitter spent more time with my kids than I did. I sat down with my husband and told him how I felt. I told him that I needed to be at home with our kids and investing more time into them. He told me that he respected my decision to be a mother before a career woman. Now I am a full-time mom!

Childhood Dream a Reality

I took tap dancing lessons as a little girl—so many years ago, I don't even remember how old I was! My mother tells me I began a tap class and then quit. As an adult, taking tap lessons has always been something I wanted to do. When our son took tap and jazz classes at the age of eight, my desire to dance was rekindled. Torrey quit after a few years, and then our daughter began taking dance lessons. Over the past eight years of my children dancing, every year I have said that I would love to take a tap class. But it never came to fruition . . . until now!

This year, as I was signing Grace up for her dance classes, I glanced over at the listings for the adult classes and saw "Adult Tap, Tuesday, 5:30." I gasped. I could do this! Grace had a different class at the same time; it would be perfect! I must say I was ecstatic but hesitant at the same time. What would Jay say? When I laid all the details out for Jay, he said, "Go for it!" I could not believe it! Laura was going to take a tap class. . . . finally!

See, I didn't ask Jay's permission per se, but I did lay out the plan as I saw it, and he encouraged me to do something I have always wanted to do. When you say *I respect you* to your wife by encouraging her to pursue her dreams, you free her to be capable.

Free Her to Be Accomplished

When I was growing up, my family didn't have money to spend on Oreo cookies, bags of chips, or frivolous snack foods. The finances just weren't available. Even if we'd had the money, my father's diabetes restricted the foods he could eat.

As a result, we pretty much ate the same food over and over again. That wasn't bad, just reality. I actually loved knowing that every Saturday night we would dine on hamburgers grilled over charcoal! When I entered high school, my mother went back to work full time. She would frequently leave dinner for me to fix when I got home from school. She would leave the recipe and the ingredients out on the counter for me so all I had to do was follow instructions. That is how I learned to cook.

When I got married, that's how I continued to cook. I fixed pretty much the same meals I'd made as a teenager. I didn't feel I could cook without a recipe. If the recipe called for some weird ingredient, I didn't make it. My culinary skills were limited to five-hour stew, chili, and of course hamburgers on the grill!

Then, a number of years ago, I discovered the Food Network. I would get on my treadmill at 4:00 every afternoon, run, and watch an hour of Paula Deen and Giada De Laurentiis. These ladies inspired me. I began watching more cooking shows and gained confidence as I tried out new recipes. My family loved my cooking, and I loved unleashing my creative side in the kitchen.

Our church has a sunrise service on Easter Sunday followed by our regular 8:30 a.m. service, a potluck brunch during the Sunday school hour, and then our 11:00 a.m. service. Bolstered by my growing culinary skills, I determined to put my love for cooking to the ultimate test. I planned to prepare prosciutto and mozzarella frittatas and take them to the potluck brunch. I would casually listen to the reviews of those who ate my little delicacies and see if my cooking passed the ultimate test of the church potluck.

To say I was overwhelmed by the response would be an understatement. I was actually embarrassed by the response. We've attended our church for nearly twenty years, and having so many people approach me saying "Where did you get that recipe?" or "I didn't know you were a gourmet cook" had me not only surprised but a bit uncomfortable. My emotions reached their zenith when Tina Weber, a *real* gourmet chef, asked for the recipe.

Later that week Jay was talking to some friends and telling them about the potluck experiment. In the midst of the conversation he called me a gourmet cook! At that moment I promised myself I would never go back to my old habits. My husband verbalizing a respect for my cooking talent changed my life.

Cooking was always something I enjoyed, but now it had become a passion, a creative outlet. Hearing those words from Jay not only caused me to realize my cooking capabilities but also propelled me toward a sense of accomplishment. Not that I was going to be the next Food Network star, but there was a thought in the back of my mind that I wouldn't be afraid to try! It was a great feeling of confidence and accomplishment.

Dictionary.com defines *accomplished* as "to be a highly skilled expert." We all have an innate desire to be highly skilled at something. When you recognize your wife's talents, you free her to be accomplished.

Free Her to Be Significant

Not only does a woman want to feel accomplished, she wants to feel significant in her accomplishments. Dictionary.com defines *significant* as "having meaning."

A woman wants her skills, her talents, her accomplishments, to make a difference, to have meaning in this world. This is an area in which many women struggle as we try to prove our importance to our families and the people around us.

When I was young, I had a friend who could do handsprings and backflips all over the backyard. She also could do the splits like no one would ever want to. But I did! I so wanted to be good at the splits and handsprings. I practiced and practiced. Alas, I had to come to the realization that God did not make this body to do those two gymnastic feats.

My sister, Sandy, is an accomplished seamstress. She inherited that talent from my mother, who is also an accomplished seamstress. My mother and sister can take any idea and make it a reality in cloth! Growing up, I always wanted to be able to sew like my mother and sister. Alas, God did not gift me with the ability to sit still long enough to do sewing of any kind. So I continued on my journey to find an area in which I could become accomplished and feel significant.

Growing up, I loved sports—softball, tennis, soccer, golf—any and all sports! On a brisk, fall day you could find me out playing football with my brothers. As a kid, I played Little League softball. In college, I played on the Belhaven College women's soccer team and was even invited to try out for the women's Olympic soccer team. As an adult I played on the church softball league until it interfered with my golf game. I love to play sports. Am I an accomplished athlete? No, I am one who plays sports. My journey continues.

My dad, Charlie, had a beautiful singing voice. Something I will always remember about my daddy was the smile on his face when he would sing in the church choir. Can I sing? Not a note! Do I ever wish I could? Always! I can honestly say there have been times I have questioned God about not giving me a singing voice. Instead, he gave me a husband with a voice like my dad's!

We all go on this journey, searching for that one area where we feel significant in our accomplishments, where others look at us with respect for our abilities. When our husbands show confidence in our abilities, we are able to rise above challenges and realize our potential.

My husband is the mechanically oriented type. He is good at seeing how things go together and rarely reads directions. In general, I am not good at those things. My dryer vent was all full of fluff so I took off the screen and got out the screwdriver, took off the parts that were blocking my access to the fluff, and cleaned it out—and I put it all back together correctly. When I told him what I had done, he said, "Wow, that's really cool that you did that yourself." I felt his respect for me.

We recently moved and I wanted to take some of the stress off of my husband. So, I offered to take over the checkbook and paying of the bills. Knowing that I struggle (putting it mildly) with mathematics, he didn't even hesitate, and handed everything over. It has been three months now. He hasn't "looked over my shoulder" once, or asked if things are being paid on time. He just trusts. Now that's respect, or foolishness!

It has taken me many years to realize that my expert skill is communicating. I have looked at others' skills and wanted what they have. I have argued with God about his ability to really know what skill to give to whom. It was not until I married Jay and we began this life journey together that I became very comfortable being a communicator. Jay has encouraged me to be the person God made me to be: a person who communicates Truth through humor and real-life stories. God gave me the skills to become accomplished. Jay's encouragement and respect for my abilities has given me the freedom to walk out that accomplishment into significance.

Don't Tread on Me!

I'm the first one to admit I was a tad bit nervous when we first started speaking together at conferences. Since I was not as confident in my abilities as Jay was in his, I would often let Jay have the lead. As we began to do more and more conferences and seminars together, I began to get requests to speak at MOPS (Mother of Preschoolers) groups and women's retreats and events. As a result of speaking alone more often, I became much more comfortable on stage.

As I became more confident in my abilities, there were times when we were speaking together that Jay would walk all over me.

Waiting for my turn to share with the audience, I would hear Jay speaking my words of marital wisdom. When he did let me talk, he would interrupt me as I was speaking—to interject words of insight that he was sure I was going to forget to say.

Needless to say, this was a frustrating situation. I would have to remind him again and again of my capabilities as a speaker. I also had to be honest with him and let him know that when he interjected himself into my speaking, I felt as if he was not respecting my part in this team. After a while he began to get the hint.

He has come a long way! I remember the first time we made it through an entire conference without him stepping all over me. I felt fantastic!

The event that brought us both full circle took place in 2007 at our Spring Conference at the Grand Hotel on Mackinac Island. Peter and Lynette Brooks have been good friends for quite some time now. Peter is the station manager of WUGN Family Life Radio in Midland, Michigan, which is a co-sponsor of our Grand Hotel events. As a result, Peter and Lynette have heard quite a bit of Jay and Laura.

Peter is a consummate professional on the air and is also very accomplished in theater. He has not only acted in numerous productions but has also directed many as well. He has literally seen it all—been there, done that.

Peter has always been very gracious in complimenting our programs and presentations. But this particular year, at the conclusion of the conference, he and Lynnette approached us with a sense of purpose. With his arm around Lynnette, Peter said, "We've been talking since the opening session, and we feel we need to tell you that this is the best program we have ever seen from you. Don't get us wrong, we've always enjoyed you, but this year it's as if you've reached a new level."

At that point Jay spoke up, "Thanks, Peter. That means a lot coming from you; we trust you and respect your opinions. I think what's finally happening is that I realize that I don't just share the stage with my wife but with one of the country's finest communicators." Peter and Lynnette turned to me and said in unison, "He's right!"

I knew I was a capable speaker. I still needed to hear Jay say it, either with words or actions. Once he stepped back and let me do the job I knew I could do, I not only felt capable but accomplished. Today, as we speak to thousands of couples, I feel like I am making contributions to the team that matter and will have significant, lasting effects.

Respect is important to every woman. A husband's respect helps his wife unlock her gifts and abilities. By communicating *I respect you* to your wife, you give her the courage to take her gifts and abilities to the next level. Not only will this help her grow as an individual, it will bolster your marriage as she hears you paraphrase

> Many women have done wonderful things,
> but you've outclassed them all!
>
> Proverbs 31:29 The Message

Helicopter Moms

Have you heard the term "helicopter mom"? I first heard this term watching the ABC news show *20/20*. Helen Johnson, author of *Don't Tell Me What to Do, Just Send Money*, said, "A helicopter mom is a mom who hovers over every state in her child's development from basically in utero through the college years and beyond."[2]

Many mothers who micromanage their children's affairs do so in an attempt to become significant through the lives of their children. This is especially true for a woman who has her first child before she has discovered her personal sense of significance. When the baby comes along, the woman may only be able to see herself as significant within the context of being a mother. But even for a mom who has a sense of accomplishment prior to having children, it is easy to get lost in motherhood. As a woman devotes herself to her family, her significance can become wrapped up in her children. And when the baby of the family grows up, a wife and mother can be confused by how challenging the process of "letting go" is.

Our son Torrey is eighteen; he is the firstborn son and oldest child. I trained him well. He does his own laundry and has since he was twelve. He put his own laundry away before he could read. I made little pictures that stuck on the drawers of his dresser so he knew where his socks, T-shirts, and shorts went.

Our daughter Grace is twelve. She is the baby of the family. I find myself doing everything for her. It has been a real struggle for me to let her grow up. I have these conversations with myself:

Grace needs to make her bed. Well, she is running a little late. I could make it for her. It really isn't that big of a deal if I do that, just this once. After all, how many more days will I have to make her bed for her?

Is that silly or what? Yet, I know every mother reading this has had similar thoughts.

We're afraid to let our children grow up because we're afraid we'll lose our significance. Gentleman, the best way to free your wife to be capable, accomplished, and significant is help her realize how important she is in your life. Fair warning, these attempts may get a peculiar reaction. Most of the time when Jay is trying to make me realize that I am the most important thing in his life—next to his relationship with Jesus—I just laugh. I laugh, not because I don't believe him, but because it is hard to accept. But with practice you'll get better at saying *I respect you*, and your wife will get better at hearing it.

Never Even Crossed My Mind

Our survey shows saying *I respect you* may be a difficult task for husbands, not because they don't want to respect their wives but simply because they have never considered the need to speak that phrase.

> Do not know if I ever have, I am embarrassed to say. I do not really have a recollection of stating to my wife "I respect you."

> I don't think I have ever stated to my wife "I respect you."

The following are four simple ways to say to your wife "I respect you."

"You're Right!"

After thirty years of marriage, Don and Gabrielle are still deeply in love. They are a delightful couple with three adult kids. Don is a very successful businessman with personality plus. He has never met a stranger and disarms even the most skeptical with his smile and charm. Gabrielle is shy and reserved and seems very comfortable letting Don take the lead.

Recently the two of them decided to build a new home on the lake. They each had their own ideas of what that house would look and feel like. Coming to the architectural table with very different personalities, perspectives, and tastes proved challenging at times.

I remember the day Don finally got it. I was on the phone talking to him and happened to ask how the home plans were coming. Don simply said, "I've come to understand the power of the phrase *You're right.*" He went on to explain he finally realized that their new house meant a great deal more to Gabrielle than it did to him. He was concerned about the size, appearance, and the quality of construction. She was concerned about creating a nest.

For Gabrielle, this house had to be so much more than a structure in which they would live and entertain. They were moving out of the house the kids grew up in, the house where family memories were made. They were moving out of a home. Subsequently this new building project needed to feel like *home.* It needed to be a place the children—and grandchildren—wanted to visit. It needed to be a place where Grandma and Grandpa could build new memories with their growing family.

By saying *You're right* when Gabrielle had a thought or idea on their new house, Don said *I respect you* in a way that made her feel capable. When he realized she did have a better feel for making the structure a home, he said, "You're accomplished in ways I am not." When Don deferred to his wife in this area, he watched her develop a sense of significance to become the grandma that his grandkids would need, as well as the wife he desired.

A husband can show his wife respect using the phrase *You're right* in little, everyday ways. From choosing a restaurant to taking ballroom dance lessons, he says *I respect you* by agreeing to go places and participate in activities that are important to his wife.

Talk to Her

Since 2006, I (Jay) have served as a chaplain for the PGA of America. Through the ministry of Fellowship of Christian Athletes, I have conducted Bible studies and prayer breakfasts at numerous professional golf tournaments. While most of the time Laura and I travel together, my chaplain duties have me traveling alone.

When I am traveling alone, no lie, I will call Laura upwards of ten times a day. These calls are one of the ways I communicate Laura's significance in my life. Let me give you a rundown of a typical day of phone calls.

5:30 a.m.: I leave the house to catch my flight.

7:00 a.m.: I call to talk to Laura and the kids before they begin their day.

8:30 a.m.: I call to let Laura know I made it safely to the airport.

9:30 a.m.: I call to let Laura know that the airplane doors have been closed and I'll be offline for two hours.

11:30 a.m.: I call to let Laura know I have landed safely at my destination.

1:00 p.m.: I call to let Laura know what golfer I had lunch with.

4:00 p.m.: I call to talk to the kids after school and to tell Laura all the different golfers I have talked with that afternoon.

6:00 p.m.: I call to report on my workout and to see what they are having for dinner.

8:00 p.m.: I call to tell Laura how the Bible study went and to say good night to the kids.

9:30 p.m.: I call to tell Laura who I went to dinner with and to find out what she is watching on TV.

11:00 p.m.: I call to discuss the shows we watched and to say good night!

So either Laura is very significant in my life, or she married a lunatic! One of the easiest ways to tell your wife you respect her is simply to communicate with her. Share the details of your day and call just to let her know you are thinking of her and you love her.

Listen to Her

Our survey responses confirmed the age-old stereotype: women don't think men listen well.

Wives don't feel respected when their husbands don't listen attentively. A husband can communicate respect for his wife just by listening to her. Sounds simple enough, but . . .

When I'm at the computer or watching TV, it is easy for me to become absorbed in what I'm listening to. Laura can start talking, but while I may hear her voice, I don't necessarily hear any of the words she is saying. Her sentences just sound like white noise. I have to train myself to act when I hear that white noise. Like Pavlov's dog, when I hear Laura's voice, my finger should spontaneously move to the TV's pause or mute button.

When I recognize Laura is speaking and I pause the television—or turn away from the computer—and turn my attention to her, I say *I respect you*. Ladies, I'll apologize now for what I'm about to say, but we are trying to be real here. Men, it can feel like an inconvenience—an interruption—to pause a TV show or computer game to listen to your wife, can't it? Let me ask this. If you have a craving for a Coke, do you hesitate to hit that pause button? No. Why would you show your wife less respect than your taste buds? We have to retrain our minds to realize our wife is not the distraction; she is the main event!

Praise Her

Before we can talk about how to do this right, we probably need to look at how a simple attempt at humor can backfire. Here is a scenario that will go down in infamy as it is told and retold to generations of Laffoons yet to come.

We were doing a sound check for an Ultimate Date Night in Caro, Michigan. Hank, the sound tech, was giving us each a headset microphone and showing us the battery-powered belt pack. "This is where you turn it on and this is where you mute it," he said.

Not thinking (my spiritual gift), I replied, "Wouldn't it be nice if it were as easy as flipping a switch with our wives? This one turns her on, this one mutes her!" Laura, who was standing right there, immediately gave me an icy stare. I was making a joke; it's what I do. For Laura it was personal and hurtful to think that I would equate our relationship to something as banal as flipping switches on a microphone.

Men, when was the last time you made a joke at your wife's expense, or aired dirty laundry at the office? Maybe you had a fight with your wife before leaving home that morning, and you are getting out your frustration with the guys. Maybe the guys in the office are engaged in locker room talk and you join in about your prowess in the bedroom. If your wife had a microphone hidden on your shirt collar, would you be proud for her to hear your office conversations?

It is important for everyone to have a confidant, a safe place to share struggles. You should have a man who will listen to your frustrations. But your relationship with your wife should not be fodder for the office cubicle.

The husband in Proverbs 31 sets the example for how we should be speaking to others about our wives:

"Many women have done wonderful things, but you've outclassed them all!" . . . Festoon her life with praises!

Proverbs 31:29, 31 The Message

Whether your wife is in another state or standing right beside you, your conversation regarding her should be filled with praise. Those who have heard you speak of your wife should expect her to be a jewel of rare beauty. When you festoon your wife with praises, you say *I respect you, I hold you in the highest regard,* and *I honor you as a wife, a mother, and a woman.* You free her from the pressures to conform to our society's view of Superwoman. You free her to be completely capable, accomplished, and significant. You free her to become the woman of God she was created to be.

Questions for Reflection

- Questions for her:
  - Is this an important phrase for you? Why or why not?
  - When your husband communicates *I respect you,* how do you respond?
  - What is the most powerful way he communicates *I respect you*?
  - Identify a particular point or story from this chapter that may help your spouse understand this need better.
  - As we walk through these different phrases, it will become apparent that you have one or two that you need to hear more than the others. Keep a tally as to the priority level you believe each one takes in your life:
    - Rank in order of priority (one through four, one being the highest priority):

- I love you
- I respect you
- I desire you
- I cherish you
- Questions for him:
  - Do you feel you communicate this phrase frequently enough for your wife? Why or why not?
  - Do you think you communicate *I respect you* in ways she understands?
  - What did you think about the four ways to communicate *I respect you* (tell her "You're right," talk to her, listen to her, praise her)?
  - Which of these ways do you do best? Which might need improvement?
  - Identify an "aha" moment in this chapter that reinforced your understanding of this need in the life of your spouse.

5

He Needs to Hear "I Need (*Blank*) from You"

I am not a mind reader!

Every husband
on the planet

The next phrase that husbands needs to hear is *I need [fill in the blank] from you.* Some women need more time, some need more affection, and some just need the trash taken out, for crying out loud. Each woman is different. So I (Jay) am not even going to try to identify that need. In truth, if you're like Laura, it would be pointless. As soon as I identified your need, it would change! What a wife needs changes every day. But what I can tell you is that it's important to understand how to communicate your needs to your man. Husbands need clear, concise communication. Men don't "get" hints. We're oblivious to what women think is obvious.

Let me share an example. I was speaking at a women's conference—the only man in a room full of five hundred women! We were all eating dinner and carrying on pleasant conversation when out of the blue one of the ladies said, "Did you see thaaaat?" I began to look around for a waiter who spilled something or an announcement on the PowerPoint screen. As I was looking to and fro to find out what *that* was, the ladies at the table exclaimed in chorus, "I know, can you believe it? Wow, what nerve!" Obviously I was missing someone or some act that every female at the table had observed. I simply cut a piece of chicken, stuffed it in my mouth, and smiled as I chewed. Oblivious!

Not Ignorant, Just Unaware

As we discussed in the *I love you* chapter, generally speaking, a woman's senses—her smell, her touch, her sight, her taste, and her hearing—are more acute than a man's. This heightened acuity, coupled with the way a woman's brain freely moves information from left to right, creates what is commonly known as "women's intuition." In our survey, wives shared their desire for their husbands to be more aware, more sensitive. Read these responses from our survey:

> I wish he would be more sensitive to the situation at the moment.

> I wish he would be more aware of the world around him.

> I wish he would just know when I need to talk.

Ladies, we wish we did too. Life would be so much easier if we just *knew* when you needed to talk! The reality is that it is physiologically impossible for your husband to be as aware of his surroundings as you are of yours. The good news is that the first step to overcoming a problem is admitting you have one. So, we've identified an awareness gap. Now, what to do about it?

Men Are from Mars, Where They Give Instructions

I can hear you laughing now. Men and instructions. What an oxymoron. Your husband is lost-er than lost and won't ask for directions. He refuses to look at the instructions that come with, well, with anything! And now I'm asking you to believe that your husband actually wants instruction?

Take it from a man who knows. We really do want instructions. We need instructions when it comes to meeting your needs.

Laura and I have a wonderful core team of people that helps us at our marriage conferences. When we get to a location to start setting up, a funny scenario begins to play out. The women just start going to work. They grab boxes and start unpacking.

Then there are the men.

"Hey, Russ, would you grab that box and start unloading it?"

"Yes, I would."

"Gene, would you start moving all of those things from over there to here?"

"Sure."

"Dan and Rickey, can you put up the display signs?"

"You bet!"

Even though these men have helped us before, they still need a little direction. They need to know precisely what it is they are supposed to do. Men are not lazy or unorganized or clueless, they simply need to be communicated with in no uncertain terms.

Trash

I walked into the house a few months ago, and Laura said these words: "The trash is full." I looked down at a trash can full of refuse and replied, "Yes, it is." What was she trying to communicate? *Would you please take the trash out?* Did she say those words to me? No. She made a statement about the trash. I agreed. I went in the other room and started watching TV.

Similarly a man walks into his bedroom, and his wife says, "Is that your underwear on the floor?" To which he replies, "It better be." His wife was not perplexed about the ownership of the

113

underwear. She thought for sure he would know what she really meant. It was a silly enough question; he simply wondered why in the world she asked it! If she would've said, "Pick up your underwear," he would've walked over and picked them up. Now he's in a quandary because he still doesn't know what to do with them.

I'm exaggerating with these examples, but do you see my point? Your husband needs you to speak in simple, direct, complete sentences. I know, many of you are thinking, *He should just know what I'm saying. Can't he see that the trash needs to be taken out? Can't he find the laundry hamper that's been in our bathroom for fourteen years?*

My question is, do you know the definition of insanity? Insanity is doing the same thing over and over expecting different results. How many times have you asked your husband if those are his boxers lying on the bedroom floor, expecting him to take the hint and put them in the laundry basket? How many times has that worked? Why think he'll suddenly be enlightened the next time? It just isn't going to happen that way. We don't get hints. We're too simple. Our brains don't have those synapses going back and forth between the left and right hemispheres. We just think and process information differently.

We Shop Differently

When I go shopping, I'm a man on a mission. I know what I'm shopping for and I'll walk directly to the store I think provides the best opportunity to bag my merchandise. If I need new underwear, I go to the Gap—best boxers on the planet. If I need new jeans, I go to Old Navy—loose fit boot cut, size 34–30 . . . okay that was a few years ago. A new shirt for the stage? Tommy Bahama, clearance rack. Simple. Direct. To the point.

When Laura goes shopping, it is a whole other story. She knows what she needs, but she wants to make sure she's getting the best deal in the mall. She travels in and out of stores, gathering information: prices, shades of color, construction of the garment, and most importantly, does she have a coupon? Then after all the information is gathered, she processes it over a Starbucks skinny vanilla latte and an Auntie Anne's pretzel with cheese. She makes her decision and returns to the proper store, only to find her item already sold. So, it's back to Starbucks for another skinny vanilla latte and to start all over! Complex. Comprehensive. Process driven.

This is also how men's and women's brains process information when we are confronted with a problem and communicate the solution. My answers are usually simple, direct, and to the point. Laura's answers are complex, comprehensive, and process driven. When you communicate with your husband, he really needs you to be simple, direct, and to the point!

A Thousand Different Meanings

Part of the problem is women often don't even know when they are dropping hints. Here is a classic example from our survey.

Annette said:

I just communicated that (*I need _____ from you*) this evening when I was trying to make some pies for a small group. I told him I just needed him to keep me company.

Chuck said:

Tonight she was making a couple of pies. It's an easy recipe, whipped cream, yogurt, and raspberries. No baking involved.

I was going downstairs to download some music. She asked me where I was going. I told her, and she just said "Oh." At that point I knew she wanted to talk.

Okay, maybe this isn't a classic illustration, because Chuck caught the meaning of this *Oh*. But most of us have not evolved that far. For most men, *Oh* means "I understand what you just said." *Oh* is simply a shortened version of "okay." There is no underlying message. Here is the proper usage of *Oh*. If I say to my son, "Torrey, the Pistons won last night," he would reply, "Oh." He understood what was said, and then we would move on.

There are others. *Do we have any plans this weekend?* is often a wife's way of saying, "I'd like to go out on a date." To her husband it's just a question about the calendar. Husbands need their wives to say, "Honey, let's go to the park Saturday afternoon."

What did you do at work? is a woman's way of saying, "I want to talk." To a man it seems like a redundant question because the answer is generally, "The same thing I did yesterday." A man needs a woman to say, "Honey, I need ten minutes of your undivided attention this evening."

A woman's girlfriends would understand those questions, and they would know that *Oh* meant, "Please, stay with me and keep me company." But men aren't wired to understand like a woman's girlfriends. Until they make a "Girlfriend Dictionary," women are much more likely to get what they want from men if they communicate using short, precise statements.

Watch Out! She's Gonna Blow!

In many ways, I am lucky that Laura doesn't drop hints. If she wants a date, she says, "Let's go on a date." If she wants to talk, she says, "Can you mute the TV so we can talk?" When communication breaks down in our house, it's usually because of what I like to call a mini-crisis. I say mini-crisis because it doesn't usually involve sickness or injury or loss of any kind. This is a sense of anticipation or a feeling of being overwhelmed on Laura's part. If you've been paying attention at all, this next statement won't surprise you in the least. This is a sense or a feeling of which I'm completely unaware. For Laura, this crisis has been building for days; yet it catches me completely off guard.

A mini-crisis typically occurs as Laura begins to think about an upcoming change in our schedule or routine. Late August is a prime example. Mid-August ushers in the beginning of school and extracurricular activities for the kids. Laura begins to think about what the kids' schedules are going to look like, what activities they are involved in, and how our speaking schedule meshes with the kids' schedules.

Being a woman, Laura has all of this information floating around in her head. This can be very overwhelming as she tries to sort through a thousand thoughts at once. A man's thoughts aren't usually that long range. They are more along the lines of, *How many books should we take to sell this weekend? Am I prepared for the talk I'm assigned to give in two days?* And most important, *What's for dinner tonight?*

For me, life is going along grand, when all of a sudden—call it a meltdown, a blowup, or a rant and rave—bam! And it usually begins something like this:

Grace's schedule is out of control, and *you don't care!* All you care about is your fantasy football team, who's leading the golf tournament, and whether or not we're having sex tonight. We'll, I'm here to tell you . . .

You get the picture. For the next number of minutes/hours I am going to hear about what an inconsiderate, selfish, self-centered *man* I am. At some point when she takes a breath, I will try to squeeze in the phrase, "How can I help?" To which Laura will reply, "Help me figure out how Grace got so overcommitted and how we can fix it!"

Now I know my assignment. Up to this point, I've been oblivious about what's going on inside Laura's head. She's made statements like, "Grace wants to take three dance classes, piano lessons, and be in swim club . . . but I just don't know . . ." To me, that's simple information. I am now abreast of the fact that Grace wants to take three dance classes, piano lessons, and be in swim club. I can't read the frustration level communicated with the phrase "but I just don't know," so I summarily dismiss it. It's not that I don't care; it's simply a phrase that I cannot interpret.

If Laura had said, "Grace wants to take three dance classes, piano lessons, and be in swim club, but I think that's too much. What do you think?" I would have responded, "Yes, that's too much." Still, I would have been the boorish pig, because knowing what I know now, in this scenario "What do you think?" really meant, "Fix it!"

On this particular day we didn't have a conversation; it was more of a monologue. I "heard about it" for the first mile and a half of our daily run. As we made our turn for home, marching orders in hand, I picked up the pace and put a plan of action into place. When we got home I went straight to my computer, put Grace's schedule on a calendar so we could see her entire week at a glance, and then printed it off. Later that night we sat our eleven-year-old down and walked her through the issues of priorities and time management as it pertained to her overburdened schedule. Clear communication is not rocket science but will produce miraculous results.

It's a Miracle

Ralph and Gigi are a lovely couple we've known for years. They love to entertain. Often on Saturday nights they will have someone over for dinner. Gigi used to spend her Saturdays hurriedly cleaning the house and fixing a wonderful meal, while Ralph sat in his chair, read the paper, and watched sports. Frustrated with the fact that Ralph should just *know* she needed his help, Gigi spent her Saturdays sighing or throwing troubled glances Ralph's way.

One Saturday it all changed. Gigi began to feel her temper boiling as she pondered her chaotic day with Ralph lounging in his recliner, reading the paper. Quickly she checked her emotions and, instead of blowing up, said, "Ralph, I need you to vacuum today." Ralph lowered the newspaper he was reading, looked at Gigi with a smile, and said, "Sure, honey."

Gigi couldn't believe it was that easy! So the next Saturday she said, "Ralph, I need you to vacuum and dust this week."

"No problem, dear," came Ralph's ready reply.

Most men really want to make their wives happy. Husbands love to see wives smile, love to hear them laugh, and love it when they are in a pleasant mood. Most importantly, husbands love to be the reason wives are smiling, laughing, and in a good mood!

When you communicate to your husband what you need using *I need* (blank) *from you*, you give him the opportunity to meet your need. Your husband gets a great deal of satisfaction out of meeting your needs and making you happy.

It Can't Be That Simple

Some women just can't believe that simplicity is the best form of communication for a man. Trust me when I tell you, it is! Because of the way a man's brain is compartmentalized, we can't connect the dots as well—or as quickly—as you ladies. Read in Liza's words how she could have saved herself a lot of anger!

> When our kids were two-and-a-half years and nine months old, they were both sick and so were my husband and me. We all felt awful. I was still changing diapers, making meals, etc., while my husband was recuperating under a blanket in front of the TV. Instead of asking him for help, I just got snarly and angry like he should have known I needed help. I did finally get the point across, and he was a big help after that. I would have saved a lot of energy if I had just asked in the beginning.

Liza connected the dots that even though both she and her husband were sick, things still needed to be done around the house. Her husband didn't connect those same dots. However, once it was pointed out to him that she needed his help, he gladly pitched in.

Physics of a Man

Contrary to popular opinion, men are not lazy. We are not watching our wives flit around the house, thinking, *Gee, I hope she doesn't ask me to do something*. In fact, we don't even see you flitting. We have a delicious spot in our brain called "Nothing." We can be sitting perfectly still in front of the TV doing nothing and thinking nothing. That is our default mode. Left to ourselves, we'll visit the land of Nothing regularly. And we'll stay there until someone kicks us out.

There is a physics principle that says an object at rest stays at rest until it is acted upon. Your husband enters the land of Nothing by default and will stay there until asked to leave. But please understand; he really doesn't mind leaving.

There is another principle that says when an object is acted upon it will choose the path of least resistance. Laura asks me to take out the trash. I agree but don't move from my chair. As I'm flipping channels, I notice Laura taking out the trash. I'm puzzled. "Didn't I say I would do that?" She shoots me her look. "I thought so, but you didn't get out of that chair."

When Laura asked me to take out the trash, she meant immediately. I heard the request and thought, *I'll take it out when I go in the kitchen to get another soda.* I was going to do it; I was just going to multitask. Ladies, if you want the trash taken out now, include that in your request. Your husband won't mind taking the trash out right now, but if you just say, "Please take the trash out," expect him to do it on his timetable.

I Can Learn

So far we've concentrated on using the phrase *I need* (blank) *from you* to help wives communicate with their husbands. But sometimes a wife will need to use this same phrase to help her husband meet the needs of her children, especially if he is a type A, driven personality like me.

One of the downsides to my driven personality is that I can be a workaholic. Aside from an occasional trip to the land of nothing, my brain never stops. Especially since the advent of the Internet, I can always think of one more "to do" I need to accomplish. Over the years I've learned that this can be a very destructive habit as it pertains to the relationships in my life, particularly my relationships with Laura and the kids.

Thankfully I married a very strong woman who doesn't have a problem being direct. Following are some statements I've heard from Laura in the past several days.

Grace needs some play time with Dad today.

Torrey wrote a new song, you need to go hear it.

We're going out for a lunch date, and I'm in the mood for a chef's salad from the Main Café.

Early in our marriage I often bristled at the direct way Laura communicated with me. Often it would come out in rebellious statements like "I don't need you telling me what to do and not to do" or "Quit trying to make me relax; I like being wound tighter than a pocket watch." Fortunately, over the years I've mellowed and matured and have come to relish the balance that Laura brings into my life when she clearly communicates the needs I should address.

In fact, once a wife begins to clearly communicate what she needs to her husband, it is like waving a magic wand. He will not only begin to meet those needs, he will also begin to get some (I said *some*) of the hints she drops. For instance, now when Laura asks, "Where are we going for lunch?" I'll respond, "Chef's salad, anyone?"

There are few things in a man's life that bring him more joy than when he helps his wife solve a problem. It is hardwired in us to want to take care of our wives and children. Just like Larry the Cable Guy, we love to "Get 'er done!" When you clearly and concisely communicate how we can help, we will dive in wholeheartedly and step up to the task.

Start Simple

Well, ladies, I (Laura) think we have our work cut out for us. Concise. What a silly word. We have a lot to say! Do they have any idea what they will be missing out on if we are concise? How can we possibly communicate all we need them to know if we only have a few words to do it in? Choose your words wisely . . . make the few you get to use good ones and hit the high points. Save your details for your girlfriends and daughters. That isn't to say that he won't listen to your stories, but when you want him to do something—when you have a need for him to meet—use few words and make them count.

Most of us like the mystery, intrigue, and romance of our husbands reading our minds and figuring out exactly what we want. But Jay has made it pretty clear that's a pipe dream. On the other hand, he also told us that our husbands *want* to make us happy. They're just asking for a little help.

Directly asking your husband to meet a specific need may be uncomfortable at first. You may find it's less awkward to start with a request that doesn't involve relationship issues but may be more of a "life" issue, like this one below:

> Not long ago, I was frustrated with the dog. I communicated that I needed my husband's help in the morning to feed the dog and let him out. (The dog listens to my husband better than me.) The outcome was very positive. I suggested a simple solution and he said, "I can do that."

As you learn how to communicate with your husband about daily tasks and routines, it will become easier and less stressful to begin talking about more intimate or relational issues, as Margaret shares.

After we had learned the concept that he can't "read my mind" from a seminar or book we had read, I expressed my need for some emotional support without the concern that he was just "interested in sex at the end of this bonding time." It's nice to know that he cares about all of me and at times we can just cuddle and hug without "strings attached."

This was a huge step for Margaret and her husband. When you begin to use the phrase *I need* (blank) *from you*, you will see amazing results.

Stranger Than Fiction

Ladies, I want to take this opportunity to debunk a misconception many of us have about our husbands. Margaret's husband's desire for sex after a bonding time is not necessarily a "strings attached" mentality. For husbands, the natural response to a time of bonding and closeness with his wife is the desire for sex. Because that is his natural response, he wonders why it wouldn't be hers too.

For your husband, a time of deep emotional connectedness naturally leads to his desire for physical connectedness. What he doesn't understand is that additional physical connectedness for you requires *more* emotions. After a time of bonding, often your emotions are spent and there are few left for the act of sex. He won't know how you feel, or what you need from him, unless you tell him. Just use short sentences with few words!

By clearly communicating that there are times when you simply need emotional support, you will find your husband more than willing to be that shoulder you can laugh or vent or cry on.

Two Little Phrases

A husband loves to fix things; that's how he's made. When you begin talking to him about a problem, he is already trying to figure out how to fix it. Sometimes you want your husband to fix a situation, sometimes you don't. I hate to be the bearer of bad news, but he can't tell the difference. Part of the difficulty lies in the fact that if he can't fix it, he isn't going to waste time on it. By virtue of the fact that you are talking about it, your husband thinks that you want it fixed.

We can't be too hard on the guys here. Sometimes we aren't even sure what we need. Remember the mini-crisis story with Grace's overburdened schedule? How much time and energy would I have saved if I had thought through what my needs were before I started that conversation, er, I mean monologue, with Jay?

Once I figure out what my needs are, I try to tell Jay what role I need him to fill in the conversation. Sometimes I want Jay to fix a problem. Sometimes I need to talk about something until I come to my own solution. Other times I know that it doesn't have an answer and I just want to rant for awhile.

Here are sentences you can use at the beginning of a conversation that will help clarify for your husband what you really want from him.

I don't need you to fix this; I just need you to listen.

This sentence will communicate to your husband that, while his *services* are not needed, his *person* is. If you've already thought this situation through and you know it has no solution, you can even tell him that. Let him know you just need to blow off some steam. Recognize this may be difficult for your husband to do at first. But when you let him know exactly what you need from him, he can be that listening ear who will hear your heart and respect your thoughts and feelings.

I really need your advice/help on this issue/problem.

Be careful not to use this sentence unless you really mean it! This sentence will typically send your man into action. During my mini-crisis, once I told Jay I needed him to fix Grace's schedule, he sprinted ahead of me. He went right home and created a plan of action.

Set Aside Your Pride

Many of us have the perception that we need to be all things to all people. But we can't. It isn't humanly possible. And, ladies, here's a secret. Your husband doesn't expect that of you. A husband and a wife are a team, so don't think you have to do it all, as this woman learned.

It was really hard for me to ask for him to help me the first two years of our marriage. I was struggling to be Superwoman and do it all. Then I went to him after watching your DVD and asked him to help and talked to him specifically about it. Now he is a great helper and will serve me selflessly.

Realize that a woman's ability to connect the dots is a great gift. When you figure out what needs to be done, don't be too proud to ask for help.

Another way pride interferes with clear communication is when we nurse hurt feelings instead of expressing our needs. Let's say you are getting ready to watch a movie with your husband. Instead of sitting in your rocker, you go sit on the couch while he finishes getting the popcorn ready. When he comes in, he hands you the popcorn and promptly sits down . . . in his recliner. You sigh loudly. He asks, "What's wrong?" You reply, "Oh, nothing," but you are certain he'll pick up on the tone. Instead, he starts the movie and eats a handful of popcorn.

At this point you have a choice. You can choose pride or you can choose to activate the truth you have learned in this chapter.

Pride will say if he cared, you wouldn't have to tell him to come sit beside you. Pride will have you pout all through the movie, wishing he would come sit beside you on the sofa and wrap his arms around you.

Truth will remind you that your husband can't read your mind. Truth will tell you he already tried to make you happy by bringing you a bowl of popcorn when he got his. Truth will have you say, "Honey, tonight *I need you to* come sit with me on the sofa while we watch the movie." Before you know it, your husband will be by your side with his arm around you. Because he loves to be the one to make you smile. He loves to be the reason you are in a good mood.

Clearly and concisely communicate your needs to your husband, and watch your relationship grow.

Questions for Reflection

- Questions for him:
  - Is this an important phrase for you? Why or why not?
  - When your wife communicates *I need* (blank) *from you*, how do you respond?
  - What is the most powerful way she communicates *I need* (blank) *from you*?

- Identify a particular point or story from this chapter that may help your spouse understand this need better.
- As we walk through these different phrases it will become apparent that you have one or two that you need to hear more than the others. Keep a tally as to the priority level you believe each one takes in your life:
  - Rank in order of priority (one through four, one being the highest priority):
    - I am proud of you
    - I need (*blank*) from you
    - I want you
    - I believe in you
- Questions for her:
  - Do you feel you communicate this phrase frequently enough for your husband? Why or why not?
  - Do you think you communicate *I need* (blank*) from you* in ways he understands?
  - In this chapter, you were challenged to use two little phrases:
    - I don't need you to fix this; I just need you to listen.
    - I really need your advice/help on this issue/problem.

    How easy or difficult would it be for you to integrate these phrases into your conversations with your husband?
  - Do you think it can be that simple? If not, why not ask your husband?
  - Identify an "aha" moment in this chapter that reinforced your understanding of this need in the life of your spouse.

6

She Needs to Hear
"I Desire You"

Men lust after women. Women lust after being lusted after.

Anonymous

Jay and I worked together in youth ministry for fifteen years, and frequently he would have to answer these questions from high-school-aged boys:

- Why do some girls dress the way they do? (translation—provocatively)
- Why do some girls move the way they do? (translation—sensually)
- Why do some girls tease? (sexually)

The answer is simple. Girls want to be noticed by boys. In the same way, husbands, wives want to be noticed by you. Not only when you desire sexual connectedness, but all the time! When you engage your wife's heart, soul, mind, and body—seeing her entire person rather than just her physical attributes—you will ignite the physical desire within her. A woman knows that you, as a man, desire her physically. What she needs to know is that you, as a husband, desire to connect with her heart and head as well.

Introducing the Significant, Non-Sexual Touch

For a man, *desire* is a sexual word. For a woman, *desire* is a wish, a craving, a longing. It does not necessarily have a sexual connotation. We desire many things: a new house, new stove, new clothes . . . chocolate! We want our husbands to desire us, long for us, to have a craving for us—but it is not always sexual in nature. Listen to this husband:

> I had the ring in my pocket, and I intended to ask her to marry me that night. I knew she would say yes, but I couldn't wait to ask her. I wanted her to be my wife—I wanted her to know that I could hardly wait to get married. Even though the wedding was months away, I desired to be "connected" to her. I could hardly wait.

Do you hear the craving in his words? Husbands, you've already played the proposal card, but you can still show your wives you desire them.

When you touch your wife in non-sexual—yet significant— ways, you communicate your desire for her. Because sexual intercourse is the culmination of intimacy for a woman (for more on this, see our book *The Spark*), she needs a day filled with you showing her that she is desirable beyond just a "grope" here and there.

"A woman needs seven significant, non-sexual touches in a day to feel loved." We love telling men this, especially in a conference setting. Without fail, we see men in the audience reach over and pat their wives on the shoulder seven times. Can you say, "Clueless"?

Exploring the following phrases will help decode what it means to communicate "I desire you" to your wife.

Significant

Non-sexual

To feel loved

Significant means "with intention": a touch you thought about making; it did not happen by chance. The touch was not accidental. If you trip and bump into your wife, that does not count as a significant touch.

Non-sexual means without the expectation of that touch leading to sex.

So a significant, non-sexual touch is one that is intentional—purposeful—but has no agenda.

Examples of significant, non-sexual touches are touches that you initiate—like holding her hand, putting your arm around her shoulder, or rubbing her back as she cooks dinner. A good-bye kiss in the morning, a big bear hug when you get home from work, and an intentional brush of your wife's blouse as you tell her how good she looks—all of these tell your wife *I desire you*.

A touch can also be non-physical. To repeat, a touch can be non-physical. Calling unexpectedly, just to say you were thinking about her, is a touch. Stopping on the way home to pick up a bouquet of flowers, or even bread, is a touch. Emailing in the morning just to tell her how much you look forward to seeing her in the evening, is a touch.

Are you keeping score here? If you do all of those—email in the morning, call in the afternoon, loaf of bread on the way home from work—you have already given your wife three significant, non-sexual touches before walking in the door! If you kissed her good-bye and gave her a hug when you got home, you have five touches under your belt before sitting down for dinner.

Women desire the connection that touching gives. Gentlemen, your wives need a hug, a kiss, a touch on the arm, an unexpected email or bouquet of flowers from you—just because! No agenda. No ulterior motive. No hoping for later. Just because.

The last phrase, "to feel loved," is perhaps the most misunderstood. Many men interpret "to feel loved" as "to be in the mood." Men, as unbelievable as this will sound, it is true: sex does not make your wife feel loved. Significant, non-sexual touches from you make your wife feel loved. You will reap untold benefits when you understand that a woman must first feel loved before she can be in the mood!

A Word from the Experts

Here are some survey responses from men who understand the importance of significant, non-sexual touches, and their very grateful wives:

> One day while she was at work I cleaned the house top to bottom. Did all the laundry and had supper on the table when she got home, complete with a rose and a note that said "I miss you."

> This is a daily process that starts with an "I love you" hug and continues throughout the day in conversation of loving her. Communicating how she looks and communicating with touch "without being asked to" (very important!) with hugs, pats here and there—not groping. Sincere contact without sexual intent.

> He tells me all the time. By brushing my shoulder whenever he walks past me, praying with me in the morning, snuggling with me after a hard day, and listening to my struggles with clients. He comes up behind me and puts his arms around me and kisses me on my neck.

> When he sends me flowers for no reason or gets me a card for no special occasion.

> It's the little things . . . touching my back as he walks by, the way he holds my face in his hands when he kisses me, the way he holds on so tight when we hug.

Boy Meets Girl

I am not sure why or how this scenario occurs, but it is very common. Man and woman meet. During the dating relationship they make a decision not to have sex. Therefore, significant, non-sexual touching becomes the physical side of the relationship: a hand held here, a pat on the knee there, a good night kiss, an unexpected bouquet of flowers, a back rub. You get the picture. The dating relationship turns into engagement and ultimately into marriage. The relationship can now be consummated with sexual intercourse. Then a strange thing happens. Sexual intercourse becomes the physical side of the relationship, and the non-sexual touching disappears. The husband is fulfilled sexually, but the wife still needs the significant, non-sexual touching to feel loved.

In the dating relationship, touching for the man is the buildup to the ultimate act of sexual intercourse. Once that becomes a part of the relationship, any touching is a means to that end result. For the woman, the non-sexual touching is an emotional and physical connection; sexual intercourse is not the intended end result. In other words, for the woman, touching is not the means to a sexual end—it is an end in and of itself. Sexual intercourse and non-sexual touch are both important to the woman, but they are seen as distinct, individual acts. This may be the only area where women compartmentalize better than men!

What's Good for the Goose . . .

I find the following excerpt from an Internet article, "Sexual and Non-sexual Touching—Body Freedom" (Self-growth.com), by Al Link and Pala Copeland very interesting:

Contrary to the stereotypes that men primarily want sexual touching and women mostly want affectionate touching, both forms are equally important for enduring, satisfying relationships. Men and women alike crave non-sexual touching. Owing as much to cultural conditioning as to physiological makeup, men are usually more accustomed to intimate touch that is sexual. But once they experience it, men love to be touched in non-sexual ways as well. Such caresses help break through times of low self-esteem, fear, and doubt. With a tender hug or gentle pat, you can give comfort and acceptance and create a strong, loving bond that goes beyond the physical. When touching is only sexual however, you might feel that you are being solicited to perform sexually or that you are valued primarily as a sexual object.

Jay has tried this ploy to show me that he needs non-sexual touches too. Whenever Grace and I come home from one of our "girls only" shopping trips, he greets us at the door with a big smile, warm hugs, and a cheerful, "You're hooooommmmme!" When I comment on how wonderful it is to be greeted like that, Jay retorts, "I would love to be greeted that way too when I come home from a 'guys only' golf trip." Guys, don't be afraid to let your wives know you'd also like your seven significant, non-sexual touches each day!

Love Languages

We often mention *The Five Love Languages* by Dr. Gary Chapman, because that one book changed our marriage more than any other. Unfortunately, many couples take the love language concept and go no further. Let me explain.

When we first read the book fifteen years ago, we decided that my primary love language was quality time and that Jay's was physical touch. However, five years ago, we reread the book and made an interesting discovery: Jay's love language is words of affirmation, not physical touch. Fifteen years ago we tagged Jay's love language as physical touch because he loved sex! Other than sex, Jay was not, and is not, really a physical touch person. The way I tell Jay I love him is to speak words of affirmation. I tell him he is a great dad and husband. When he hits a great golf shot, I let him know. But words of affirmation do not fulfill him sexually.

In the same vein, I am a quality time person. I love to spend time with my family. I love to go out to lunch with my husband, go shopping with my daughter, and sit and listen to my son play his guitar. Quality time is definitely my love language. However, I still need to be touched. Even though physical touch is not my love language, those significant non-sexual touches are an important connection to my husband.

Too often, we discover and speak our spouse's love language but fail to understand the importance touch plays in our lives. No matter what love language you speak, non-sexual touch is vital for a woman, and sexual intercourse is essential for a man.

What It Ain't

We've seen what significant, non-sexual touches look like. Now here's a peek at what they don't look like!

> A few times in the past, I tried to surprise her by coming home early and meeting her for lunch for a little afternoon delight. The last two times failed miserably. She went to get her nails done and the other time she stayed at work.

> [He shows me he desires me] when he wants sex.

Let me (Jay) ask, do you see where these men went wrong? Guys, we are only fooling ourselves. Women know when we are playing them for our own needs. It is not a compliment to our wives when we want to have sex with them. They expect that. When we try to pass off foreplay as a significant, non-sexual touch, it's a huge turnoff to our wives.

He seems to always be pawing at me.

Nope [he doesn't say "I desire you"]. It's "I want you," and at least once a night. Just sounds so cheap!

This usually happens most days, but the only communication is, "Let's go to bed" or "Let's get naked!"

Unfortunately it has been more of a groping affection—grabbing and possessing me rather than alluring me. He sometimes gets this "look," but I would prefer massage or non sexual affection and gentle words of love and kindness.

In order to communicate *I desire you* to your wife, we must place a guard in three different areas of our life.

Guard Your Head

So, guys, we've got some work to do. We have to be on guard against our sexual nature when it comes to showing our wives we desire them. I did not say bottle it up and throw it out! I said guard against it. Simply put, that means guard against sex being the first thought when communicating desire to your wife. Remember, for her, desire means you love her and long to connect with her heart, mind, and soul.

We men have to make deliberate, conscious choices on a daily basis to put up our guard. I find the definitions for *guard* intriguing:

1. to keep safe from harm or danger; protect; watch over
2. to keep under close watch in order to prevent escape, misconduct
3. to keep under control or restraint as a matter of caution or prudence
4. to provide or equip with some safeguard or protective appliance, as to prevent loss, injury

When you guard against your sexual impulses, you protect your wife and yourself from danger. You keep a close eye on your choices in order to prevent misconduct. You restrain your natural lust as a caution. You build safeguards into your life to prevent the loss of your marriage.

Men, God has given us an innate drive to protect our wives. Nowhere in your relationships will you demonstrate that God-given manliness more than when you protect your marriage by guarding against your sexual impulses. Our friend Bruce understands what it means to be on guard:

I thank the Holy Spirit that I love my wife and only my wife. My thoughts of desire and passion are focused on her and no one else. I can't do that myself, but I can with the help of the Holy Spirit.

We must guard our heads against two inevitable changes that will occur in our wives: physical changes and emotional changes.

Her Physical Changes

You may have heard this saying before: a woman marries a man hoping he will change; a man marries a woman hoping she will never change.

But she will change. Her weight will fluctuate. She will change her clothes with the styles. She will change her hairstyle and probably even her hair color! She will grow up and mature. Your wife will change.

When Laura and I met in the summer of 1984, she weighed a whopping 110 pounds! Actually, she was too thin. During her last year at college she struggled with habits that could have easily led to an eating disorder. Fast-forward twenty-five years . . . let's just say those thoughts that plagued her in college concerning food intake are a thing of the past!

Today, Laura looks healthy. Her weight isn't the only thing that's changed: baggy sweats replaced jeans as her favorite pair of pants, she's grown her hair out, and she wears makeup daily instead of just for special occasions. She is not the same woman I married twenty-five years ago—physically or emotionally.

Her Emotional Changes

Guys, if you think PMS is bad, wait till menopause comes knockin'. Laura has nicknamed this season "mental-pause" because something happens hormonally that causes women to pause mentally. They become forgetful, and their brains don't work as quickly.

Those same hormones also affect our wives emotionally. They become overly sensitive to the words they hear. Words spoken at any moment—by any individual—can cause Laura's sensitivity meter to go up, down, or way off the chart!

During this highly charged time, carefully guard the thoughts that run through your head, like, "I liked her better when she was not screaming." Significant non-sexual touches can work wonders during this challenging life phase.

Here are some comments from women whose husbands have obviously guarded their heads:

> He communicates verbally how he desires me, but again I sometimes have a hard time really believing that. I am overweight and always feel inadequate regarding my physical attractiveness, because I know this is very important to him.

> There's never been a time that I haven't felt desired by my husband. There have been times I've felt undesirable, but he's always made me feel desired.

> ALWAYS! Although it can be annoying to hear it all the time. I am thankful that my husband does desire just me. He makes me feel beautiful on the days I feel the worst. When I am having a hormonal insecure day, he seems to say the right thing . . . most of the time.

This excerpt from Dr. Laura Schlessinger's blog is the most impressive example of guarding your head through the years. Some may not like his choice of words, but folks, the facts are the facts! Women change!

> Making love to my seventy-five-year-old lady is wonderful, and I have the thrill of making her enjoy her sex. (Wow.) My greatest honor was to be invited into her body so long ago. She was all mine at eighteen and still is. As the subtle changes came along in her life and body, I was happy, because I knew that I was part of each of them. She still has great looking "boobs" and a beautiful behind. I love handing her the towel as she steps out of the shower with that great welcoming smile.

> Dr. Laura blog reader, September 15, 2008

What I love about this man is his perspective that he was a part of the changes in his wife. I firmly believe that this gentleman saw these changes as subtle because he had guarded his head years ago. Guarding your head keeps your marriage safe and speaks *I desire you* to your wife.

Guard Your Heart

The second area we need to guard is our hearts. You communicate *I desire you* when you consciously guard against giving your heart away to anyone or anything other than your wife.

When men speak of guarding our hearts, we immediately think we are talking about an affair. You may think, *As long as I'm only sleeping with my wife, this doesn't concern me.* You couldn't be more wrong. Certainly infidelity is one way men give away their hearts, but there are many others. Some of them are subtle but still very damaging to a marriage.

Besides adultery, a husband can give his heart away in various ways. He can give his heart to his job. He can give his heart away to a hobby. He can give his heart away through pornography.

Guarding your heart is a matter of restraint and equipping each other with some safeguards to prevent loss of the marriage.

Get That Thing Outta Here

A Victoria's Secret catalog comes into our home every month. For a long time Laura would just leave it out on the dining room table. At the time, we had a thirteen-year-old son in our house. It never occurred to Laura how tempting that catalog would be to the men in her home.

One day I finally told Laura, "You know, we've got a thirteen-year-old in the house; you ought to put that away." She didn't let me get by with laying all the blame on our son. "Oh, do you ever look at it?" Caught like a deer in the headlights, I sheepishly admitted, "Yeah, you might want to keep that away from me too."

Laura would have never known the temptation I faced if I had not confessed it to her. But, not only did I communicate my temptation, I also suggested some safeguards. Now when the catalog comes in the mail, Laura looks through it and then puts it in the trash. It cannot lie around our house, even in a pile of other magazines. It will be found!

In sharing my temptation and constructing safeguards to have the temptation removed, I communicated my desire to only have eyes for Laura. That is something every woman needs to hear and feel from her husband.

Something's Gotta Give!

Guys, we can obviously give our hearts away through pornography or to another woman. We hear a lot about this issue, and it is certainly wrong. What is more difficult to define, and therefore harder to remedy, is the issue of when a husband gives his heart away to his job.

We have friends whose marriage is on the rocks because of their jobs. Ken had a fantastic offer to work a job that was out of town. When he first accepted the job, the plan was for his wife, Sue, and the kids to move to that town after school was out for the summer. During that first year, they developed a workable routine. Ken was gone during the week and home on the weekends. That first year turned into two years, and then three. Sue and the kids stayed at home, and Ken went to work out of town.

Needless to say, that workable routine became habit over a three-year period. Now their marriage is suffering. Here is where something's gotta give! Ken's job is a great one, but so is Sue's.

Ken's new job is in a great town. Home is great too. There are many options in this situation to make this marriage work that would involve both Ken and Sue giving. In order to communicate *I desire you* to Sue, Ken needs to be willing to say, "I am willing to do whatever it takes to make this marriage work, even if that means quitting this job and finding something different at home." There is no job more important than the relationship you have with your wife.

These men in the following examples show how to communicate *I desire you* to your wife by taking time out from your job or normal routine:

From time to time I make arrangements to have the kids spend the weekend with Grandma and Grandpa. We go out to dinner, maybe a movie, an after-dark walk, and that sets the mood just right.

The time that stands out in my mind was when he left me a note in my underwear drawer that told me to pack an overnight bag and that he would be picking me up soon. We spent the day together. Then he took me to a fancy dinner and a beautiful hotel where chilled champagne and a hot tub were waiting. He had taken the time to plan everything including who would take care of our children. It was very romantic.

He had been running 24/7. And our time was being crowded out. He called and said, "I'm coming home this afternoon and shutting the phone off for a couple of hours and we are going to pretend we are on that much-needed island vacation. Turn down the bed, I'm there in ten!" I laughed and giggled as I went to unplug the phone.

Usually I do the planning for our anniversary celebrations. This past year, however, my husband took care of it. I was thinking dinner and a movie, but he wanted to get away with me. He booked us a room at a "couples only" hotel and made all the arrangements for a wonderful anniversary.

Guard Your Hormones

In chapter 7, I (Jay) will explain the male hormonal cycle. But for right now, I'll share with your wife that, unlike her twenty-eight-day cycle, you have a seventy-two-hour cycle. While sex is never far from any man's mind, science is showing that after seventy-two hours without sex, hormones begin to act on our brains, causing us to experience heightened sexual urges. We aren't animals; we can control these urges. But as we approach and pass our seventy-two-hour mark, the hormones influencing our brain make control more challenging.

With your seventy-two-hour cycle and your wife's twenty-eight-day cycle, there will be a lot of days when your urges don't match. How you respond to your wife during these times demonstrates your desire for her . . . not only your desire for her physically, but your desire to connect with her.

> He usually does this by coming up behind me, kissing the back of my neck, and caressing me. He tells me how beautiful I am and what features have caught his attention. All the while, he is reading my responses. If I am not responsive, he doesn't push to get what he wants.

While there will be more times that you are the one having to delay gratification, there may be times when you are satisfied and your wife initiates sex. When you accept your wife's sexual advances, you tell her *I desire you*. Your wife is very well aware that you are a sexual creature. When you say "no thanks" to sex, she feels completely undesirable. This is especially true for those marriages (research indicates about 20 percent of all marriages) in which the wife has a higher sex drive than the husband.

Men, we guard our hormones when we are sensitive to our wives' responses and advances. When we guard our heads, our hearts, and our hormones, we say *I desire you* to our wives in ways we never have before!

Questions for Reflection

- Questions for her:
  - Is this an important phrase for you? Why or why not?
  - When your husband communicates *I desire you*, how do you respond?
  - What is the most powerful way he communicates *I desire you*?
  - Identify a particular point or story from this chapter that may help your spouse understand this need better.
  - As we walk through these different phrases, it will become apparent that you have one or two that you need to hear more than the others. Keep a tally as to the priority level you believe each one takes in your life:
    - Rank in order of priority (one through four, one being the highest priority):
      - I love you
      - I respect you
      - I desire you
      - I cherish you
- Questions for him:

- Do you feel you communicate this phrase frequently enough for your wife? Why or why not?
- Do you think you communicate *I desire you* in ways she understands?
- Identify an "aha" moment in this chapter that reinforced your understanding of this need in the life of your spouse.
- You were challenged to guard your head, your heart, and your hormones. Which of these three is easiest for you to guard? Which is under most attack?

7

He Needs to Hear
"I Want You"

I want you to want me.

Cheap Trick, 1979

Before your eyes glaze over from the title of this chapter or you summarily dismiss me as a boorish pig, I (Jay) want to ask you to hear me out. Let me explain the truth.

I don't know why God made us the way he did, but I can guarantee this, there is not one part of the female body that a man doesn't find sexy. I will confess right now that I can get sexually turned on by Laura's ankles, for crying out loud. She can have on baggy sweatpants, no makeup, and her hair under a baseball cap, but when she brushes up against me, one hundred thousand volts of sexuality course through my veins. The energy is electrifying!

Your husband wants nothing more than to give every one of those one hundred thousand volts to you. Deep in his heart he desires to lavish you with romance, affection, and love.

A husband needs to know that his wife wants him. Wanting him is very different from him desiring you. Yes, we're talking about sex now. I know this is one of the touchiest subjects on the planet. It's unbelievably awkward to talk about. But trust me, your husband is thinking about it, so we might as well talk about it.

For about 80 percent of marriages, the husband's sex drive is higher than the wife's. To those who married a man with a very high sex drive, he seems to be nothing but a pervert because all he thinks about is sex. The other 20 percent of women think

151

they've got a defective model because he rarely thinks about sex. No matter where he falls on the spectrum, from the man who can never get enough to the fellow who thinks sex is only for making babies, your husband needs to know that you want to be with him sexually.

"Sexy" Is in the Eye of the Beholder

A couple of years ago, I had laser surgery on my eyes. For two weeks after the LASIK surgery—to prevent damage to my eyes—I had to put on little plastic goggles so that I didn't rub my eyes while I was sleeping.

One night after I put on the goggles, I realized I had forgotten to brush my teeth. So I went back into the bathroom, goggles still in place. While I was brushing my teeth, I looked in the mirror and marveled at how much I looked like a superhero. I began to make "manly" poses in the mirror, dreaming of what special superhero powers I might possess. Would I have X-ray vision, superhuman speed, or the ability to fly? Maybe all three!

All of a sudden I heard Laura say from the bathroom doorway, "Heyyyy." She had caught me. She had been watching me make all my poses and now she was cracking up. I had to respond. What would I do? Without missing a beat—in my deepest, sexiest voice—I said, "Honey, ever made love to a superhero before?" She immediately replied, "Every night, dear, every night." Oh my goodness, talk about one hundred thousand volts!

Guess what? We didn't have sex that night. Why not? I just needed to know Laura would. I just needed to know she wanted to if I did. In fact, I didn't need sex for three days. Want to know why? Because to her, I'm Jay-Man, the superhero!

Male PMS

Ladies know a lot about cycles. They know that about every twenty-eight to thirty-two days, something's coming. They've even given a name to the week of preparation before it gets here: PMS—a warning to men that it's coming.

Women, can any of you adequately explain that process to a man? No. Things are changing in your body, hormones are raging, and you have no control, am I right? You can't stop it; you can only hope to contain it. All of a sudden you wake up one day feeling bloated, feeling fat, feeling cranky—and the world's going to know about it.

Ladies, inside of your husband, there is also a cycle. Research is beginning to show that, just as with a woman, a man has a hormonal cycle that occurs within his body. For the average man this cycle occurs every seventy-two hours.

Every seventy-two hours, the man experiences an internal buildup. Hormones begin to attack his brain, making him obsess over issues that were only a blip on his radar two days earlier. Under the influence of those hormones, his imagination is taken to new heights. Just like a woman, a man has no control over his cycle. His feelings and emotions well up in him and need a place to go.

At this point in the cycle, a husband deeply wants all that pent-up energy to go solely to his wife. Think about that. From your husband's perspective, this is the ultimate expression of love, and he wants to give it all to you.

When he feels unloved, when he feels unwanted, that trapped energy begins to go places that are unhealthy for a marriage. Are we saying that you need to give sex to your man every time he wants it? That is between you and your husband. We are saying that there are very real forces in place here.

"Life Is Like a Box of Chocolates"

Imagine a bar of Hershey's chocolate. Are there certain times of the month when all you want is chocolate? How many, like Laura, have a secret stash in the house that no one else knows about? How many have uttered the words, "Step away from the chocolate"? For some, it's not chocolate, it's salt or ice cream or all three! You have no clue why you crave, but the craving is real.

For most husbands, that urge for "chocolate" is with him twenty-four hours a day and peaks every seventy-two hours. A good friend of mine once commented, "I wish it was as simple as a candy bar. Then instead of being sexually frustrated, we'd just be fat." For some of your husbands, there just wouldn't be enough chocolate in the world!

Hungry?

We all have different sexual appetites. In many marriages the husband's sexual appetite is different from the wife's. Walking through marriage, couples will discover their spouse's "hunger" level. Couples need to work out reasonable and fair expectations. And as soon as they do, age or illness or medication will mess it all up. Then they'll have to work out the details all over again. It will not, however, change the fact that a man needs to know that his wife wants to be with him sexually.

Why? Because knowing his wife wants him is part of what makes a husband feel like a man. As we have discussed in other chapters, it is not and should not be the only way he feels like a man, but it is an integral part. We have often said that, for a woman, when all is right in the world (kids in bed, doors locked, chores done), then all is right in the bedroom. For a man, when all is right in the bedroom, all is right in the world. A quote from our survey says it best.

> The last time I was over the top on this was after an emotionally draining time when I expressed how much I needed intimacy with her to right my world.

This man accurately articulates how for a man, even in the midst of crisis or trouble, sex can be a huge stress relief.

The Difference Between "Willing" and "Want To"

Somewhere between the ages of thirty-five and forty, after Grace was born, Laura and I experienced a hunger level change. Due to some medical issues, Laura's doctor recommended we not have more children. We agreed the best solution was for me to have a vasectomy.

With the fear of pregnancy gone and our lovemaking skills improving, we both found our sex life quite enjoyable. Then, as life would have it, it all began to change again. I wish I had a dime for every sexual adjustment we've gone through in our marriage!

As I progressed into my mid-forties, I no longer wanted to "just have sex." I wanted our encounters to be "lovemaking." One night, feeling a bit frisky, I began putting some time-tested moves on Laura. I asked, "Do you want to make love tonight?" Laura responded "Yeah, I'm willing." It was as if she had sucked out all the oxygen from the room. I was devastated. I couldn't reconcile the words *lovemaking* and *willing* in my brain. I rolled over and began to pout like a baby.

For me, and many men, there is a big difference between *willing* and *want to*. I am willing to take out the trash. I am willing to wash the cars. I am willing to eat just a salad for dinner. I want

155

to play golf. I want to watch sports. I want to eat steak. *Willing* is an obligation. *Want to* is a priority.

After Laura coaxed me out of the fetal position, we began to talk about my issue with her choice of words. She understood how important the difference in meaning of those two words was to me, particularly as it pertained to our sex life. I asked her to eliminate the word *willing* from her sex vocabulary. Once again, a simple adjustment made our sex life all the better.

A Wise Woman Once Said . . .

Our friends Stacey and Dottie Foster live in Detroit and pastor Life Changers International. Stacey is a dynamic speaker. Dottie is a beautiful woman with an extra dose of wisdom.

I was with the Fosters on a mission trip to Guatemala. We were there on behalf of Compassion International, seeing the projects and children that Compassion works with. After a day of touring the Compassion projects, Stacey, Dottie, and I had dinner together.

We spent the meal talking about the day, laughing with each other and catching up on our respective ministries. As the conversation turned toward Celebrate Your Marriage and the couples we were working with, we began to talk about the common challenges couples face. Naturally one of those common challenges is sex.

Dottie said, "Men need to understand that, for women, there are four weeks in every month." All of a sudden I was a bit confused and wondered, *Aren't there four weeks in every month for a man too?* At this point Dottie made herself perfectly clear. She elaborated, "Because of the hormonal changes in a woman, each one of the four weeks has its own distinct personality."

Week one: I think my husband is a pretty good guy. I think he's a good father and a good provider. I'm proud to call him my husband. I like him, but that's about it.

Week two: I can't keep my hands off my husband. I think he's the most wonderful man on the planet and I can't get enough of him. He just drives me crazy (in a good way). All I want to do is be "with" him.

Week three: I can't stand my husband, or any man on the planet for that matter. He just drives me crazy (in a bad way).

Week four: I feel like my husband is my buddy. Because of my monthly visitor, we're just roommates.

The lightbulb went on in my head. Instantly I replayed the years of our marriage and could identify this exact pattern. There were times when Laura was willing but not enthusiastic. She even offered a polite, "Not tonight, dear." Then there were times when—and I'm not complaining—it was like I was a sex god. She couldn't keep her hands off of me. While I didn't know (or care!) why, I certainly wasn't going to fight it. Then, without warning, bedtime bliss turned into "You're such a pig, all you think about is sex." I began to recognize that this signals the impending week of "hangin' with my buddy" in baggy sweatpants. All of this occurred in mind-numbing, rapid-fire succession!

A wife's changing sexual personality is all very confusing to husbands. We know the woman of our sexual dreams is located somewhere inside of her. We see her from time to time. Our frustration is that we need our sex kitten every seventy-two hours, but she only comes out to play one or two nights a month. We spend the rest of the month searching for our lost tiger. In our search, we're made to feel like we only want her for her body. We need to know that our sex kitten wants us; she is just playing a spirited game of hide and seek, waiting to purr with delight when she's found.

Business 101

We were doing some counseling with Tyler and Kris. We have known and loved Tyler and his family since he was in middle school. We were really enjoying getting to know Kris through the counseling process. They were young, had a beautiful young daughter, and had encountered a very rough patch of life over the previous two years. Tyler had lost his dad in a hunting accident, and his dad's death had really taken a toll.

While walking through some of their struggles, we discovered that some of the external issues of life had wandered into their bedroom. Tyler had grown a little detached, particularly about some of the business struggles his young company was having. Tyler's detachment made Kris a bit hesitant to respond in the bedroom.

You could feel the tension in the room, and I felt a need to lighten the mood. "For a man," I said, addressing Kris, "when all is right in the bedroom, all is right in the world." Kris was very young, and like most young women, she really couldn't believe that life for a man could be that simple.

I explained to Kris how when a man is loved by his wife sexually, when she abandons herself to him in the bedroom, that literally unlocks a dragon slayer. Whatever the dragon in Tyler's life, Kris could play a huge role in him slaying that monster. At that moment, I simply said to her, "Kris, when you intentionally decide to communicate to Tyler that you want him sexually, you will be amazed how it spills into every aspect of your life. If you don't believe me, take a look at Tyler." She turned to see his face beaming, a grin stretched from ear to ear. Tyler, a former NCAA Division I football player, replied enthusiastically, "Babe, there's nothin' I wouldn't tackle!"

Unleashing Your Dream Husband

Your husband knows you want him to be a leader. He knows you want him to connect with you and the kids. He knows you want him to listen when you speak. He *needs* to know that you want him sexually. Telling your husband *I want you* unlocks his potential to be the leader, communicator, and listener you desire him to be.

Quite frankly, ladies, we are complicated creatures. Kris had a difficult time understanding that life for a man could be so simple, because life for a woman isn't that simple. Men really may have the shorter end of the marriage stick. Books are filled with the intricacies of the female mind. Most guys need just two things: sex and food. If food wasn't required to sustain life, you could sum up the male in just one word.

In other chapters of this book, we explore aspects of the husband-wife relationship that are important to a healthy marriage, but none of them has as big of an impact on your husband as telling him *I want you* sexually.

So, if all our husbands need to be happy is sex, why do we have such a hard time giving it to them? Just like our husbands, we need to place a guard over three important areas of our lives.

Guard Your Hormones

Dottie's story illustrates how our hormonal cycle impacts our ability to say *I want you* to our husbands. At least two weeks out of the month, weeks three and four, our hormones scream, "Leave me alone!"

We need to recognize how our cycle affects us. Every woman is different. Being aware of our cycle and the effect it has on our body as well as our personality is of great importance when saying *I want you* to husbands.

As Jay shared, a man's hormones have just the opposite effect on him. His hormones cause him to be attracted to his wife. But imagine if a husband's male PMS caused him to withdraw physically. How would a wife feel if he didn't give her a single significant, non-sexual touch for two weeks? Particularly if you suffer from PMS in a difficult way, then you better be saying *I want you* to your husband very loudly in weeks one and two!

Our hormonal changes often wreak havoc on our emotions, leading us to the second hurdle we face in saying *I want you* to our husbands.

Guard Your Heart

As I experience hormonal changes, my emotions can get the best of me. I often find myself angry for no reason. It's like an out-of-body experience! I am seeing myself screaming at children I love dearly for no apparent reason other than they exist!

A screaming wife is not what puts Jay in the mood. Nor does screaming say to him *I want you*. I have had to identify these emotions in my life and do my best to stop them before they escalate into a scream fest at the Laffoon house. With Jay's help, I identified the times of the month they were most likely to happen and began to anticipate the coming of these emotions. I schedule fewer activities on those days and I block off time throughout the day to decompress. Just three minutes of deep breathing has an amazing effect on my ability to remain calm and focused. A cup of Earl Grey tea before the kids get home can prepare me for the frenzied onslaught that is soon to approach. Beginning my day with reading and prayer has a huge effect on how the rest of the day goes.

As I began to get a handle on this, I was better able to take care of the emotions before they erupted. I communicate *I want you* to my husband by guarding my heart, the seat of my emotions, against ugliness.

While guarding our hormones and heart is key, there is one final piece that is critical.

Guard Your Head

Guarding our head is pivotal in saying *I want you* to our husbands. While our hearts are the seat of our emotions, our heads are the seat of our wills. Desire is a decision. We expect our husbands to lay aside their sexual nature and give us seven significant, non-sexual touches a day—without expecting anything in return. Ladies, we need to reciprocate and make the decision to want our husbands sexually whether or not we are in the mood. The following excerpt from Anahad O'Connor in the *New York Times* illustrates this point.

For almost a decade, researchers at Pfizer Inc. struggled to show that Viagra, the company's male impotence drug, could enhance sexual function in women.

Last month, they gave up.

Countless tests on thousands of women made it clear that the little blue pill, though able to stir arousal, did not always evoke sexual desire. Viagra's failure underscored the obvious: when it comes to sexuality, men and women to some extent are differently tuned. For men, arousal and desire are often intertwined, while for women, the two are frequently distinct.[3]

Once again science shows how differently men and women are wired. This also demonstrates the important role a woman's mind plays in sex. Our mind is our greatest asset when trying to communicate *I want you* to our husbands. We just have to make it work for us!

When Jay first began his speaking career, I did not travel with him. I would stay home, go to work every morning, and take care of our kids and the house in the evenings. Sometimes he would be gone several days . . . well past his seventy-two-hour quota! When he walked through the door, he was ready for some TLC. After days of acting as a single parent, I was ready for a vacation. The problem was that my vacation didn't include sex.

Our lifestyle interfered with our intimate life. Our needs weren't in synch. My needs were based on shouldering the sole responsibility for our home and needing a break. His needs were under the influence of hormones. How many times have I expected my husband to make accommodations for my PMS? The least I could do was reciprocate the courtesy!

So I decided to prepare for his arrival. Before he got home, I prepared my mind for sex. I decided we would have sex as soon as the kids were safely stowed away, and I decided I would like it! And an amazing thing happened. The more I focused on our intimacy upon his arrival, the more I looked forward to it!

Sometimes you can plan to be in the mood. Sometimes he catches you off guard. When that happens, you can let him know you need a moment to get yourself ready for him. Go to the restroom, brush your hair, brush your teeth, and remind yourself that this amazing hunk of a man cannot wait to give every one of his one hundred thousand volts of sexuality to you!

When you guard your hormones, heart, and head, you remove the obstacles to telling your husband *I want you*. When you decide to desire your husband, you say *I want you*. A husband who feels wanted leads his home and loves his family in powerful ways.

Questions for Reflection

- Questions for him:
  - Is this an important phrase for you? Why or why not?
  - When your wife communicates *I want you*, how do you respond?
  - What is the most powerful way she communicates *I want you*?
  - Identify a particular point or story from this chapter that may help your spouse understand this need better.
  - As we walk through these different phrases, it will become apparent that you have one or two that you need to hear more than the others. Keep a tally as to the priority level you believe each one takes in your life.
    - Rank in order of priority (one through four, one being the highest priority):
      - I am proud of you
      - I need (*blank*) from you
      - I want you
      - I believe in you
- Questions for her:
  - Do you feel you communicate this phrase frequently enough for your husband? Why or why not?
  - Do you think you communicate *I want you* in ways he understands?
  - Identify an "aha" moment in this chapter that reinforced your understanding of this need in the life of your spouse.
  - You were challenged to guard your head, your heart, and your hormones. Which of these three is easiest for you to guard? Which is most under attack?

8

She Needs to Hear "I Cherish You"

I am my lover's. I'm all he wants. I'm all the world to him!

Song of Songs 7:10 Message

Men know what men want, and women know what men want. Men want women. For me, Jay, this has always raised the question, "What do women want?" To which Laura answers, "Women want it all!" For a woman, *I cherish you* is the one powerful phrase that encompasses all of the others. You show your wife you cherish her when you love her, respect her, and desire her. In other words, for your wife, being cherished is the culmination of love, respect, and desire. Women will feel cherished when they have it all!

To understand this need, men first must understand the dream. The dream of your wife's fairytale wedding began with Cinderella. Most little girls have played out their dream wedding dozens of times before they even think boys are cute.

To a little girl, the dream means an exquisite white gown with a long flowing train, elegant floral arrangements, and an unforgettable bridal entry down a cloth-lined walkway flanked by bow-ladened pews. As the girl begins to entertain the notion that boys are actually part of the human race, her romantic notions of a beautiful wedding turn to hopes of finding her soul mate, a man to share her dreams, schemes, and moonbeams.

As that little girl grows into a woman, she realizes that the dream is all about the man. Every woman longs to share her life with a man who cherishes her. A woman feels cherished by her man when:

- he shares his life with her
- he can think of no one else but her

- he desires her
- he needs her
- he holds her in high regard
- he cannot live without her
- he nurtures her
- he is tender with her

Most importantly, when he shouts to the world, "I have forsaken all others for her!"

In the Beginning . . .

Regardless of the wedding vows you used, traditional vows give us a glimpse of what it means to cherish.

> Will you love her, comfort her, honor and keep her, in sickness and in health, for richer, for poorer, for better, for worse, in sadness and in joy, to cherish and continually bestow upon her your heart's deepest devotion, forsaking all others, keep yourself only unto her as long as you both shall live?

When a husband cherishes his wife, he shows her she holds his deepest devotion, purest loyalty, fondest affection. *I cherish you* says a husband is committed to his wife above anyone or anything. Saying *I cherish you* is not something to be taken lightly!

Weaker Vessel?

> Husbands, likewise, dwell with them with understanding, giving honor to the wife, as to the weaker vessel, and as being heirs together of the grace of life, that your prayers may not be hindered.

> 1 Peter 3:7 NKJV

I (Laura) for the life of me can't figure out why on earth would we choose this verse to talk about cherishing your wife. When most women hear this verse, their knee-jerk reaction is, "Weaker vessel, I'm not the weaker vessel. In fact, the longer we're married, the more I think I can whip his scrawny behind!" This verse can stir up some controversy, can't it?

As a woman, something about this verse never seemed quite right to me. Something seemed out of place. When I think of a weaker vessel, an object of scorn sooner comes to mind than a cherished object. So I did a little digging. Do you know what I've found out as I've looked at this verse in the original Greek text? "Weaker vessel" isn't at all what our Western culture would interpret it to be. When this verse was written, "weaker vessel" actually meant "fine china."

So now, let's reread the verse using that paraphrase.

Husbands, likewise, dwell with them with understanding, giving honor to the wife, as to *fine china*, and as being heirs together of the grace of life, that your prayers may not be hindered.

What a beautiful picture. Men, God sees your wives as fine china. He expects you to treat them accordingly. As a matter of fact, he feels so strongly about this, he says if you don't "treat them with respect as fine china," your prayers will be hindered.

God thinks of your wife as fine china. Delicate. Rare. Beautiful. This is a great concept to keep in mind as you consider how to cherish your wife. Leo shares how he cherishes his wife:

I bought a curio cabinet that I set up to display pictures and memories from the time that we met until present day.

Wow, this man really understands how to cherish his wife as fine china! But don't rush out and buy a curio cabinet just yet. Leo's china treatment won't work for every woman.

The Perfect Pattern

Did you go shopping with your wife to pick out your wedding china? Do you remember the mind-numbing variations of patterns you had to look through before deciding on the "perfect pattern"? Well, think of every woman as a unique china pattern. No two of us are the same. The good news is that you have already selected your "pattern"!

Now you get to study your pattern. Like a hunter studies his prey, its habitat, its diet, its sleeping pattern. Apply that same sleuth mentality to learn the intricacies of the swirls, dots, and colors that make up your wife's unique pattern. This is your mystery to solve. You get to figure out how your wife wants you to cherish her.

Another Picture of Cherish

Lyrics from this often-used wedding song paint a picture of what it means to cherish.

> You are flesh of my flesh
> Bone of my bone
> There's no one closer
> You are flesh of my flesh
> Bone of my bone
> We are one
>
> I do pledge my life to you
> Forever and always

I will take good care of you
And shower you with praise

Others try and separate us
But they don't have a chance
No one else can take your place
No not even one

I do give my life to you
Today and every day
I will stand right by your side
Whatever comes our way

I have searched and searched for someone
Who'd make my dreams come true
Nowhere else on this earth
Is there anyone like you

The storms of life can blow and blow
But they won't knock me down
We'll stand the test
The test of time
'Cause we stand on holy ground.[4]

Leon Patillo

Let's take a closer look at some of the statements in this song to give husbands a better idea of what it means to cherish their wives.

No One Closer

Okay, men, we know when most of you feel closest to your wife . . . it would be when you make love. Now, you need to know that your wife feels closest to you when you are "in tune" with her thoughts, desires, and feelings.

For example, when Jay finishes a sentence for me, and I say, "That is exactly what I was thinking!" Or when he suggests going out for a chef salad at the Main Café, and I exclaim, "I have been craving that for two days." Or when he senses and acknowledges that I am overwhelmed with life right now and asks, "What can I take off your plate?" It is in those moments when I know that there is no one closer.

Lisa shares how her husband cherishes her:

When he tells me I am his backbone, that is his way of saying he cherishes me.

I Pledge My Life to You

Marriage is promising your life to someone forever and for always. No take backs!

When a husband pledges his loyalty to his wife with a "no take backs" mentality, she feels safe and secure. Early in our marriage, Jay and I looked each other in the eyes and said, "Divorce is not an option." With those spoken words, Jay communicated to me his lifelong pledge that no matter what happens along the journey, "I am here."

Marriage is not a fairytale. At times, the journey may be less than what we expected. A husband must continually pledge his life to his wife, not his kids, not his mama. Every day, no matter the cost, your wife needs to hear you say, "Today, I pledge my life to you."

I Will Stand Right by Your Side

This phrase speaks of loyalty. All the time, but especially during times of crisis, your wife needs to know you've got her back.

Every marriage will go through storms. A wife needs to know her husband isn't going anywhere. She needs to know that he will be right there by her side no matter what.

When the crisis comes, your wife needs to hear *I cherish you*, as this man communicated to his wife:

> Last week, again after a particularly hectic day of trying to help a grieving daughter through a painful move, I told my wife how much I cherish the time we have together. . . . She means more to me than anything in this world.

Over the last eighteen months, I (Laura) have had numerous friends who have been diagnosed with cancer. Through radiation, chemotherapy, surgeries, and the uncertainties that accompany this dreadful disease, every one of these women's husbands have been there. These men have not left, they have stood by the side of their wives through the crisis of this disease.

From the moment we say, "I do," husbands and wives are partners together in this journey of life. How exciting to take this journey with your spouse!

> I work full time and my husband has been quite ill for the past three years. He is also a wonderful cook. God has been good to him/us and he is doing well right now. A couple weeks ago I came home from work, and my husband had fixed a wonderful supper, had flowers on the table, and a beautiful card that simply stated thanks for being by my side. It doesn't get any better than that.

When you stand by your wife's side through the good and the bad, you tell her *I cherish you*.

Nowhere Else on This Earth Is There Anyone Like You

Men, do you remember how excited you were when you realized she was the one? How nervous you felt when you asked her if you were *her* one? Then she said, "Yes!" In that instant, you found a partner to walk this journey with.

But then the mortgage comes . . . and the car payments . . . and the kids. Where does the time go? Yet you are still on the journey. When was the last time you let her know you're glad she's still walking it with you?

> I told my wife that after being away at a leadership retreat without her. I called her at the break to say I missed my partner.

Your wife is your partner, someone to walk with and share life with.

Recently, Jay flew to Regina, Saskatchewan, to speak at a fundraising dinner for a Christian school. During one of his frequent phone calls home, he made this statement: "If I had my way, I would never speak on stage without you at my side, ever again." When I heard those words, I wanted to reach right through that phone and kiss him full on the lips!

In twenty-five years of marriage, I have only heard Jay use the word *cherish* once. And that pertained to a family vacation memory. But throughout our marriage, in moments such as this, he could not communicate it any clearer.

Who Sings?

Gentlemen, here is the essence of what I want you to understand about the song on pages 170–71. This song is written from a man's perspective. The man sings it to the woman. Any husband who says these words to his wife, whether through actions or actual words, finds a woman who is cherished!

Now for the really good news: a wife who is cherished develops the enduring qualities of beauty, strength, and wisdom.

Beauty

We have all watched as a bride and groom face one another and gaze into each other's eyes. The bride's face is luminous. She radiates a beauty that comes from being loved.

Similarly, I have looked into the face of a woman whose marriage is falling apart. She looks hardened, bitter, and hurt. She may have attractive physical features, but her sparkle is gone. Her beauty is overshadowed by her pain.

We have heard it said that before a woman turns forty, her beauty is largely due to the way she has treated herself. After a woman turns forty, a woman's beauty is largely due to the way her husband has treated her.

I don't know if this can be scientifically proven, but from my real-life observations of married people, I find this to be right on!

Our daughter Grace is named for a very beautiful woman. Grace Wolgemuth served as the first lady of Youth for Christ from 1965 to 1973 when her husband Sam served as president. I, Laura, met Grace in February of 1997 while attending Youth for Christ's Midwinter Staff Convention. Now, eighty years old, Grace was stately, charming, and would be described by anyone as absolutely beautiful. Her husband Sam was the consummate gentleman and doted on his bride of fifty-seven years as if they were newlyweds.

In the course of one of our meetings, we were instructed to circle up and pray with those around us. Grace was sitting in front of Jay and me, and she turned around and said, "May I pray with you two?" From the moment Grace's prayer flowed from her mouth, I was amazed at the inner beauty of this woman. She exuded a love for her Lord that I had never seen or heard before. I knew in an instant that the baby I was carrying was to be named Grace.

Gentlemen, cherish your wife and you will give her an enduring beauty.

Strength

God is not silent on the matter of drawing strength from one another.

> Two are better than one,
>> because they have a good return for their work:
> If one falls down,
>> his friend can help him up.
> But pity the man who falls
>> and has no one to help him up!
> Also, if two lie down together, they will keep warm.
>> But how can one keep warm alone?
> Though one may be overpowered,
>> two can defend themselves.
> A cord of three strands is not quickly broken.
>
> Ecclesiastes 4:9–12

A wife draws strength from a husband who cares for her, nurtures her, and protects her.

When a man cherishes his wife, he is committed to her success in every aspect of their lives. He supports her career, her activism, and her friendships. He undergirds her in her roles of wife and mother.

When Jay and I both read Suzie's statement below, we felt as if she had hit the nail on the head!

I wish [men] would see their interactions with women as an opportunity to form a "blessed alliance." I believe God designed us to work together, not to compete against each other. When we join together in a common cause, each offering our gifts, the best outcome is achieved.

A husband's devotion gives his wife the strength to be the woman God created her to be. A woman who is cherished has a confidence in her femininity. A confident woman is a strong woman. She is confident in who she is, where she is going, and how she is going to get there!

Wisdom

When I ponder enduring wisdom, my mind automatically goes to Proverbs 31.

Charm is deceitful and beauty is vain, but a woman who fears the LORD, she shall be praised.

Proverbs 31:30 NASB

A wise woman has more than just beauty and charm, she fears the Lord. Wisdom ultimately comes from the fear of the Lord.

The fear of the LORD is the beginning of knowledge; fools despise wisdom and instruction.

Proverbs 1:7 NASB

While the beginning of wisdom comes from relationship with God, Proverbs also shows us that a husband's love causes his wife to be wise and strong.

Her children rise up and bless her; her husband also, and he praises her, saying: Many daughters have done nobly, but you excel them all.

Proverbs 31:28–29 NASB

When a husband praises his wife in front of others, he is cherishing her by demonstrating his confidence in her abilities. A husband's confidence in his wife gives her the wisdom to make decisions concerning herself, her marriage, and her children. The natural outflow of wisdom is kindness and peace.

She opens her mouth in wisdom, and the teaching of kindness is on her tongue.

Proverbs 31:26 NASB

For where you have envy and selfish ambition, there you find disorder and every evil practice. But the wisdom that comes from heaven is first of all pure; then peace-loving, considerate, submissive, full of mercy and good fruit, impartial and sincere. Peacemakers who sow in peace raise a harvest of righteousness.

James 3:16–18

All of these amazing qualities are a result of wisdom.

Is there a man out there who does not desire a woman full of beauty, strength, and wisdom? Practice the following three actions regularly and you will be amazed at the fruit!

Chivalry Is Not Dead

As our son ventured through his elementary years, we began to teach him a little more about respect, beyond your basic "please" and "thank you." We taught him to look adults in the eye when he spoke to them, take off his hat when he came into the house, and hold the door for his mom and sister—or any woman, for that matter.

One day as he was walking into church, he stopped to hold the door for the women who were entering. An older woman took the door from him and said, "You don't need to hold the door for me, young man. You go ahead of me." He said, "No, ma'am. My mom and dad taught me that I am to respect you and I'm going to hold the door for you." He sat and fought with this woman because she wouldn't enter the church. Later he said, "I don't get it." And quite frankly, neither do we. Most women would love for you to hold the church door, car door, house door, or any door for them!

Opening the door for a stranger is called a random act of kindness. Opening the door for your wife is called cherishing her. You don't have to buy your wife the Hope Diamond to show you cherish her. Simple, everyday actions say *I cherish you.*

> Be more thoughtful all the way around. Not that I'd want gifts or anything, just "thoughtful." Help with your coat, open your door, pick up something you drop, tell you that you look nice, just stuff. Thoughtful of others.

The first action to practice: don't let chivalry die!

Non-Sexual Touches—Your New Best Friend

In the "I desire you" chapter, we discussed non-sexual touches. I (Jay) understand this is a difficult concept for us men. Our minds and bodies are programmed to see sex everywhere. But let me tell you why non-sexual touches should be your new best friend. Not only do your non-sexual touches communicate *I desire you* to your wife, but they also communicate *I cherish you*. Two for the price of one!

It gets better. These non-sexual touches don't just let your wife know that you desire and cherish her; they also bring back mystery and romance to your relationship. Guys, believe me, I know how hard it is to understand non-sexual touches. But hear me out on this. Your gentle, thoughtful touches not only make your wife feel more valued than a Ming vase, they also leave her with a sense of intrigue. You become your wife's very own James Bond!

In the process of writing this book, Laura and I naturally did a lot of discussing about our thoughts and how to verbalize them. As we were discussing the importance of non-sexual touch, as it pertains to both *I desire you* and *I cherish you*, I listened intently. Laura shared that sometimes in order for a woman to feel desired and cherished, as we said before, the non-sexual touch needs to be "just because," with no agenda. In other words, I can't leave her a romantic note in hopes of getting lucky later that evening. I have to leave the note just because I cherish her. I'm not hoping to get anything out of this; I'm just doing it because I love her.

Later that afternoon, Laura picked up our daughter, Grace, from school and took her to a dance class. They were gone most of the afternoon and into the early evening. While they were out, I bought Laura a bouquet of fall flowers and placed them on the kitchen counter with a note that read, "Just Because." Yep, I was on a roll . . . no moss growing under my feet!

Later Laura shared that she'd had a week filled with intense writing, school schedules, and travel. She was feeling a little overwhelmed and in need of some tender loving care. The flowers and note made Laura feel cherished.

When you understand your wife's thoughts and feelings without explanation, she feels cherished. When you show that you understand her feelings with a non-sexual touch, you say *I cherish you*. Non-sexual touches are the fleshing out of *I cherish you*. Here are some other specific examples of non-sexual touches that communicated *I cherish you*.

I show that I cherish my wife with calls, cards, flowers, and gifts.

There are times I feel so low, and all he has to do is take me in his arms and hold me close. He doesn't have to say a word . . . but I know deep inside he loves me. That says "I cherish you" to me.

When he holds me close at night, not wanting anything in return.

A call. A card. Some flowers. Holding her close. Yes, cherishing your wife really is that simple. When you give of yourself in a non-sexual way, without expecting anything in return, you show your wife you cherish her.

After Laura saw the flowers and read the card, our daughter Grace turned to her and said, "I hope I marry a man just like my daddy!" When you cherish your wife, you show your daughters how they should be treated by their husbands. When your daughter begins to look for the man of her dreams, you will have set the bar high.

The second action to practice: remember the importance of non-sexual touch.

Make a New Compartment

My man brain has little compartments. Every day I check off my compartments:

- Have I gotten my work assignments done?
- Have I exercised?
- Did I check the mail?
- Have I updated my fantasy football team?

When we were dating and newly married, cherishing Laura came naturally. It was an outpouring of the newfound love I had for her. While my wife is not another task on my to-do list, the busyness of life can push aside, or completely close, the compartment in my brain that longs to cherish her. Many of us need to re-open that compartment that says:

- Have I cherished my wife?

Cherishing is found in the day-to-day activities of life. When you gas up your wife's car, you cherish her. When you hold your wife's hand as you walk down the street, letting the world know you are with her, you cherish her. When you get up to get yourself a cup of coffee and bring her one also, you cherish her.

The final action to practice: make that new compartment in your daily mental checklist.

Live Like a King

King Solomon, the wisest king who ever lived, knew how to cherish a woman.

> I'm spoiled for anyone else! . . . I am my lover's. I'm all he wants. I'm all the world to him!
>
> Song of Songs 7:6, 10 Message

That is how your wife wants to feel. She wants to know you have abandoned all others—that you only have eyes for her and you are spoiled for anyone else. Follow in the footsteps of a great king . . . cherish your wife!

Questions for Reflection

- Questions for her:
  - Is this an important phrase for you? Why or why not?
  - When your husband communicates *I cherish you*, how do you respond?
  - What is the most powerful way he communicates *I cherish you*?
  - Identify a particular point or story from this chapter that may help your spouse understand this need better.
  - As we walk through these different phrases, it will become apparent that you have one or two that you need to hear more than the others. Keep a tally as to the priority level you believe each one takes in your life:
    - Rank in order of priority (one through four, one being the highest priority):
      - I love you
      - I respect you
      - I desire you
      - I cherish you
- Questions for him:
  - Do you feel you communicate this phrase frequently enough for your wife? Why or why not?
  - Do you think you communicate *I cherish you* in ways she understands?

- At the beginning of this chapter we shared that feeling "cherished" is the culmination of the other three phrases. When a woman feels loved, respected, and desired, then she feels cherished. On a scale of one to ten, ten being high, how cherished does your wife feel?
- Identify an "aha" moment in this chapter that reinforced your understanding of this need in the life of your spouse.
- Of the three ways mentioned—chivalry, non-sexual touches, or making a new compartment in your man-brain—which do you think will help your wife feel most cherished?

9

He Needs to Hear
"I Believe in You"

I have a dream.

Dr. Martin
Luther King Jr.

Earlier we talked about the phrase *I'm proud of you*. *I'm proud of you* acknowledges a husband's past and present accomplishments. *I believe in you* speaks to a husband's future pursuits.

When a woman says to her man *I believe in you*, she is expressing her confidence in him. Speaking that phrase is like telling her husband, "Honey, there is no person on this planet I would rather stand by, sit by, and sleep by than you."

Say *I believe in you*, and your man will begin to change. Quotes from our survey say it best:

> She tells me constantly. She is my biggest fan. And you better not say anything bad about her man!

> My wife calls me her "Knight in Shining Armor." She believes I can do anything.

These wives understand the power of believing in your husband.

The Twenty-First-Century Man

Our society tends to downplay the immense pressures on men today. We know there are also incredible pressures on women living in the twenty-first century. Since this chapter is about husbands, we want to help you understand some of the pressures men face. The Gallop and Rasmussen polls track politics and national trends. We want to narrow our focus: what pressures affect the twenty-first-century churchgoing man? George Barna, the leading pollster when it comes to Christians and life in the church, is an expert at getting statistics relevant to the Christian community.

Barna found that for every ten men in your church . . . Wait, read that again. For every ten men in your church—not for every ten men in your town, not for every ten men where your husband works, not even for every ten men in your neighborhood. These survey results are based on every ten men *in your church*. When you go to church this Sunday, look around. Find ten men. Of those ten men, nine will have children who leave the church. It's true that both fathers and mothers feel pain when a child does this. Both are plagued with questions of inadequacy. "What did I do wrong?" This statistic has your husband asking, "What kind of legacy have I left?" In regard to our kids, more is caught than taught, so a man begins to question his performance as a father and spiritual leader in the home.

A man sees his children as a reflection of himself, the purveyors of his legacy. For a man who has a hard time expressing his faith verbally, the reality of this statistic can be devastating. A father is left wondering if there was more he could have said or done to keep his kids from losing their faith.

Job Satisfaction

Of those same ten men, eight will not find their jobs satisfying. Now, as a woman, you may be working and not find your job satisfying, either. We understand that's a tension both husbands and wives may have to endure. But when a man spends his life at a job he does not find fulfilling, when he gets up every morning and goes to his unrewarding job because he has a responsibility to provide for his family, that man questions if his life will ever make a difference. He begins to question his future potential.

Listen to the impact these wives had on their husbands' futures, as it pertains to their jobs.

My husband needed to know I believed in him when he interviewed for a position that required more experience than he had. I reminded him that despite his lack of qualified work experience, he did have personal experiences and the drive to be a dedicated and professional employee, which should count for a lot. His work ethic and abilities would take him to the place he deserved to be. He got the job, but I wasn't the least bit surprised, just very proud and happy.

My job responsibilities at work had been changed and I had been passed over for a promotion I'd been hoping for. I was in quite a funk. She was there to encourage me and lift me up. She helped me understand it wasn't that there was anything wrong with me and that God had something better lined up.

When my husband wanted to start his business—leave the company he was with and go on his own—I told him I believed in him and he could do anything he put his heart into.

When a man knows his wife believes in him, he looks to the future with strength and optimism, unafraid to pursue his dreams.

Overextended Credit and Financial Pressure

Of those same ten men, six will pay the monthly minimum on their credit balances. We don't have to tell you that our country has seen its economy shaken to the core. Easy credit has allowed many men to overextend their household budgets in hopes of providing a better life for their wives and children. Facing financial pressures not only buries your family financially but also buries any hope of significance deep inside your husband.

Pornography

Five of those ten men have a major problem with pornography. Five out of ten . . . that is one out of every two men in your church who have a major problem with pornography. Other statistics show that one out of every four pastors has a problem with pornography. Based on my own perspective as a man, as well as from what I know of my friends and the people that I come in contact with, let me speak frankly. If Barna eliminated the word *major* from this survey question, I believe this statistic would read, "Ten out of ten men in church have a problem with pornography."

Here's why I believe that. A man cannot turn on the television, go to the movie theater, drive down a freeway with billboards, or read a magazine without seeing images that a Christian man should not see. Because of the way we're wired, those things stay with us. It's as if they're imprinted on our minds forever. Yes, your husband is absolutely responsible for putting a guard on his eyes. But in the world we live in today, to completely avoid these stimulating images, a man would have to gouge out his eyes.

I know there are women reading this book who struggle because they know their husbands are dealing with this issue, and they don't think they measure up as women. They look at themselves and say, "I don't look like that; I don't act like that. I couldn't look like that; I couldn't act like that. He'll never want me." But hear me, hear me! Your husband longs to desire only you. It is a battle. It is a war. What your husband needs more than anything else is for you to come alongside him and help him fight the battle. When you do, your belief in him gives him a vision of winning this war!

Divorce

Four out of ten men at church will get divorced. In addition to the husbands and wives whose lives are shattered, divorce affects one million children each year. Divorce and its ugly realities have hit us all. We would be hard-pressed to find anyone whose life has not been affected by divorce. Whether a relative, co-worker, or friend, we all know someone who has been scarred.

During the Saddleback Civil Forum on the Presidency, Rev. Rick Warren asked presidential candidate John McCain, "What is your biggest moral failure?" Without missing a beat McCain answered, "The failure of my first marriage." For a man, divorce is the ultimate admission of failure.

A wife who believes in her husband through tough times can be the lifeline to escaping this statistic.

> When my husband had his affair and after four months of emotional trauma, he wanted me to take him back. I laid out a few conditions, one being counseling for as long as it takes no matter how much it costs. He didn't think he could handle reliving everything, but I told him I believed in him and us and after what we'd been through we could make it.

Biblical Worldview

Only one man has a biblical worldview. For over ten years now the Laffoon family has advocated for Compassion International, an outstanding organization that is dedicated to releasing impoverished children from their plight. Our son Torrey actually got us involved with the organization.

I am embarrassed to say that prior to getting involved with Compassion, I never really cared about poverty, which is arguably the most significant issue Christians have before us. Matthew 25:31–46 lays out God's expectations for his children and the eternal consequences.

This passage of Scripture is about judgment day. On this day, Jesus will gather all nations together and "will separate the people one from another as a shepherd separates the sheep from the goats" (Matt. 25:32). What is the qualifying question? What did you do for the least of these? I will never forget reading the first chapter of James as I sat on a plane traveling to my first mission trip with Compassion International. I read in verse 27, "Religion that God our Father accepts as pure and faultless is this: to look after orphans and widows in their distress."

For most men this is a tough passage to swallow as we try to provide for our family but also recognize our God-given mandate to care for "the least of these."

Balancing Family and Work

Finally, all ten will struggle to balance family and work. Every job has its pros and cons. Regardless of their occupation, for most men the biggest con is time missed with their kids. I love my job. I love communicating with people and making them laugh. And yes, I enjoy the spotlight. As much as I love what I do, anxiety fills my heart in the days before an extended period of travel, because I know I will be completely away from my kids. News of a flight or weather delay feels like an arrow piercing my heart.

Men feel immense guilt when our responsibilities at work keep us away from those we love. No matter the profession, balancing family and work is tough. As we wrestle to strike the right balance, we need to hear that our wives believe in us.

My husband started med school less than a month after we were married (twenty-two years ago). He faced many classes and hospital rotations, some easy and some more difficult. When the stress or doubt would creep in, words became very powerful. Just knowing he had someone at home who believed in him and was waiting for him at the end of the day gave him strength. Simple words like "You can do this!" when spoken by someone who loved him and believed in him reached his heart and helped him move forward.

Strength for the Fight

From unfulfilling jobs to overextended finances to moral failures to unmet expectations, men in the twenty-first century engage daily in face-to-face combat. When a wife speaks the phrase *I believe in you*, she gives her man the courage he needs to slay the internal and external dragons he fights each and every day.

He Has a Dream!

What is your husband's dream? Maybe it's to run a business. Maybe it's to use a particular gift or a skill to earn a living. Maybe it's to restore a car or boat or house. I don't know what it is, do you?

My dream was always to be on stage. I can remember being at concerts or events when I was a kid and thinking, *That would be one of the most fun jobs in the world.* In high school and college I vacillated between "Christian Rock Star" and "Funny Speaker

Guy." I loved to entertain, but more importantly I saw entertainment as a means to communicate a message. Whenever I dreamed about my future, it was always on stage.

As I said earlier, my first year out of high school I knew I wasn't ready for college, so I traveled full-time with a Christian rock band. We would perform at high school assemblies during the day, singing and playing the latest pop hits. Then we would invite the students back that night for another concert. We'd play Christian rock music and give our testimonies. It was a grueling year—performing three and four shows six days a week—but I loved every minute of it!

All through college and my early years as a youth minister, I sang and made people laugh. By the late eighties I began to get requests to speak at conferences and youth retreats. By 1994 I was gone two or three weekends a month.

During this time my good friend and mentor Ken Davis kept urging me to go full-time with my speaking and comedy. I certainly wanted to follow Ken's suggestion. But I didn't have the confidence that God had given me the abilities to make a living on stage.

In 1995 Ken wrote a book *Fire UP Your Life* about living with nothing to prove, nothing to hide, and nothing to lose. He gave me and Laura each our own copy. On the inside of mine he wrote, "Time to take your speaking career to the next level!" His words were encouraging but still made no impact on my future. I wasn't willing to risk my family's financial security to pursue my lifelong dream.

On the inside of Laura's book Ken wrote, "Fire UP your life! Or at least build a fire under Jay." Shortly after reading Ken's encouragement, Laura pulled me aside and said, "It's time you dive headfirst into speaking." I had never heard those words from her and, at first, I didn't believe her. After two weeks of conversations and answering all of my "what if's," Laura had finally had enough. "Why can't you believe in you the way I believe in you?"

That single sentence changed my life forever. Her words were all the courage I needed. Knowing that my wife believed in me and the gifts I had been given tipped the scales and allowed me to start pursuing my childhood dream. In my first year speaking full-time I grossed eighteen thousand dollars. After expenses and taxes, my net pay was less than half of what I had been making as a youth minister. Fortunately Laura had a good job with benefits, and the speaking contracts were starting to come in for the next year. Now, almost fifteen years later, I've had the privilege of providing for my family by communicating God's truth through music, comedy, and the spoken word.

My dream would never have happened without Laura speaking the simple phrase *I believe in you*! For years my parents had said it, audiences had said it, friends and mentors had said it, but when *she* said it, the weight of her words tipped the scales and propelled me into the life I'd only dreamed about living.

Women can't imagine the power they wield in the lives of their husbands. Uttering the phrase *I believe in you* to your husband unlocks the shackles of self-doubt and launches him into the destiny he was meant to live.

The Power Behind the Words

The great thing about my wife—and the real secret to making this phrase so powerful—is that after she said it, she backed it up with her actions. There have been times over the last decade and a half when she could have complained that there was too much month at the end of the money. Instead, she found ways to make the budget work. There have been times when the calendar in the coming months didn't show many speaking opportunities. Instead of stating the obvious, she always reassured me that this was my calling and God would supply a way. There have been countless weekends when she lived as a single parent. Instead of telling the kids, "Wait till Dad gets home," she would discipline and correct them with grace and love.

Your husband needs to hear the words *I believe in you*, but he also needs to see that sentiment lived out in your actions.

A Great Place to Start

Maybe you feel awkward about speaking these statements out loud to your husband. Maybe you don't know where to start without it feeling contrived or pretentious. Here is some great advice from an anonymous respondent to our survey.

> When my husband and I started praying together nearly a year ago, I realized that when I talk to God about my husband while he's with me, I am able to express things I would feel odd just saying out loud under other circumstances. Praising God for his growth as the leader of our household, thanking God for choosing him as my husband, praising God for the work he is doing in my husband are all ways I communicate *I believe in you* to my husband.

Step 1: Discover His Dream

You may know your husband's dream. You have talked at length, and he can articulate his dream well. If this is your situation, feel free to skip to step 2! But for many men, their dream is locked inside. They are still that little boy too afraid to let others know what they really want to do. To Jay, admitting he dreamed of being on stage and desired the spotlight seemed arrogant and prideful. To me, those desires were the natural outflow of his God-given talents.

In her book *Eat Well, Live Well*, Pamela Smith, RD—a nationally known nutritionist, energy coach, culinary consultant, and best-selling author—has a list of dreamers' questions.[5] If your husband is unsure of his dream, help him walk through these questions:

1. I am passionate about . . .
2. If I didn't have to worry about money, I would work at . . .
3. I believe I was put on this earth to . . .
4. I will be remembered by future generations for . . .
5. Imagine being on your death bed, and a reporter asks you to reflect on your life. What have you done to bring fulfillment to yourself and others? What do you still want to do?

Discovering your husband's dream is the first step in communicating *I believe in you.*

Step 2: Develop His Dream

So, you know his dream. Now comes the fun: create and implement a plan for making that dream come true!

Working together as a team, ask this question: "If money was not an issue, what would we like our life to look like in five years?" Now, working backward from that vision, create measurable and attainable mini-goals to help you reach your vision.

We initially had a four-year plan for Jay to transition from his corporate position with a national ministry organization to his lifelong dream as a self-employed speaker-entertainer. That plan gave us security in the form of dependable income and benefits while Jay's speaking engagements grew to a level that could provide for our family. Through circumstances beyond our control, God condensed our time frame just a little—from four *years* down to four *months*! The prospect of being so totally dependent on God for every aspect of our lives—all at once—was scary but also exhilarating!

Develop your plan but keep in mind that God may have a better plan. Be willing to follow his lead.

Step 3: Defend His Dream

You have discovered his dream and created the plan. You are on your way to living your dream. Ready yourself for speed bumps and road blocks. When our four-year plan turned into a four-month plan, we had a choice to make. We could surrender and retreat to a life that seemed safe and comfortable or we could forge ahead with the accelerated plan and grab hold of our dream.

Just like us, you will face obstacles on the way to your dream. Expect the challenges; they may slow you down (or speed you up!), but they won't throw you off course. We had committed to each other that we would do whatever it took, even if that meant flipping burgers, to make Jay's dream a reality. Count the cost, commit to the cause, and then get creative.

One of the first ways we overcame our obstacle of a shortened time line was that Jay took a position with Michigan Schools in the Middle as a presenter of its curriculum and programs. Jay would travel during the week, conducting teacher in-service training. This schedule left his weekends free to take ministry engagements. God provided this part-time position to help bridge the gap created by our shortened time frame.

Our obstacle was time. Your obstacle might be others questioning your judgment, unsupportive family and friends, illness or injury issues, current financial debt, or a lack of education. The list of potential obstacles is endless. The reasons to abort your dream will often be more plentiful—and seem more logical—than the reasons to pursue your dream.

Once you discover your husband's God-given dream and devise a detailed plan of action, you must determine this is a dream worth fighting for. With everything in you, defend his dream against all obstacles.

Believe!

In ancient Greek, the word *believe* means "to live by." It's been said that God made Eve from Adam's rib so that we would know that husband and wife were meant to walk side by side. *I believe in you* is not just a catchphrase to get husbands off the couch and motivated to move. *I believe in you* is a commitment to the direction and path that you two have chosen to walk together.

Some of you might be thinking, *This is great for him, but what about my dreams?* We would never imply that a wife's dreams always come second to the husband's dreams. However, I will tell you that I always dreamed of being a published author. When Jay got his dream, my dream wasn't far behind. Funny how God works those things out, isn't it?

Questions for Reflection

- Questions for him:
  - Is this an important phrase for you? Why or why not?
  - When your wife communicates *I believe in you*, how do you respond?

- What is the most powerful way she communicates *I believe in you*?
- Identify a particular point or story from this chapter that may help your spouse understand this need better.
- As we walk through these different phrases, it will become apparent that you have one or two that you need to hear more than the others. Keep a tally as to the priority level you believe each one takes in your life:
  - Rank in order of priority (one through four, one being the highest priority):
    - I am proud of you
    - I need (*blank*) from you
    - I want you
    - I believe in you
- Questions for her:
  - Do you feel you communicate this phrase frequently enough for your husband? Why or why not?
  - Do you think you communicate *I believe in you* in ways he understands?
  - Do you know your husband's dream?
  - Reflect on ways you can tangibly help him reach his dream.
  - Identify an "aha" moment in this chapter that reinforced your understanding of this need in the life of your spouse.

10

Things We'd Like to Change

I love you just the way you are.

Billy Joel, 1977

Yeah, right.

Jay Laffoon, 2009

As part of our survey, we asked men and women what they would change about the opposite sex. We put one condition on their response: they could not say they would want to change anything that is part of the opposite sex's nature in general. For example, they could not say, "I wish my wife desired sex more." They had to list an item that their spouses actually had the ability to change.

Interestingly enough, both sexes overwhelmingly wanted change in the area of communication. Simply put, the women wanted men to talk more, and the men wanted women to talk less. Fortunately, the responses didn't stop there. Our respondents took their answers to a deeper level. Women wanted men to talk more in a specific area, notably feelings and emotions. Men wanted women to talk less in a specific area, notably complaining and criticizing.

Women's Survey Says . . .

Here are a few examples of how women wish men would change:

- Willingness to listen—not to try to solve our problems for us but just to listen
- Listening skills
- Listen more attentively

- Open up more; share their feelings

Right up front, women don't think men listen well. This correlates directly to all four powerful phrases. A wife does not feel loved when she thinks her husband does not care enough to listen. She does not feel respected when he does not value her thoughts. She does not feel desired when he does not talk all day but wants sex at night. A woman who does not feel loved, respected, nor desired, certainly does not feel cherished.

Homework

From time to time, our daughter, Grace, comes home overwhelmed with the amount of homework she has for the evening. She simply cannot comprehend getting all that work done in the limited amount of time she has before bed. Translation: "I am not going to have time to watch TV today!"

One particular Thursday evening, Grace was overwhelmed, and everyone in the house was going to know about it! Being a good dad and not wanting to see my daughter in pain, I offered to help. Her request was simple: "While I finish my math, can you help me find these last five words in my word search?"

Valiantly I took the word search, found the five words, and circled them. As Grace was finishing her math, I handed her the completed word search. The look on her face was pure devastation. "I wanted your help; I didn't want you to do it for me! I wanted to circle the words." I looked at Laura and said, "She is no longer a little girl; she is a full-blown woman!"

Grace was simply asking her dad for some help with her problem. As a dad and man, I heard her ask me to fix her problem. Grace did not feel like her wishes were respected. As a result, our time spent together solving the problem was not a cherished father-daughter relationship moment.

Drilling Deeper

Women reveal how they'd like their husbands to listen and share.

- "I guess I would want them to be more willing to delve into the deeper levels of communication. They appear to be very willing to discuss superficial issues not only with women but with each other. It all goes back to men allowing themselves to be vulnerable enough to share on a deeper level."
- "I would have them share their feelings more openly and be able to listen to our feelings with more understanding."

Sharing on "deeper" emotional levels makes a woman feel cherished. In these quotes, the women express that when a man listens intently, he communicates to his wife that she is valued above all else. When a husband listens to his wife, he communicates that he deeply values what matters most to her.

Men's Survey Says . . .

Here are some examples of how men would change women:

- Complain less
- Criticize less
- Nag less
- Judge less

We were amused at how different the quotes are: the women's answers were wordy while the men's responses were concise and to the point! These are pretty direct answers. The transparency and consistency of the men's answers amazed us.

When a wife complains, criticizes, and nags she reveals her heart of doubt. A husband who is criticized feels as though his wife is never proud of him. Complaints cause a man to question what it is that women really need from him. A nagging wife is never attractive to her husband, and her doubt makes him question her belief.

The School of Complaining

Laura and I have talked at length about complaining, and Laura is *not* a complainer. Quite the opposite. I often tell her that I don't think she complains much at all. As I've asked her to observe other women—the tone and inference in their language—she has received an interesting education in how women complain. Trust me, your husband picks up on this just as quickly as Laura and some of the men from our survey:

- "Women enter into relationships thinking they can change a man. The approach is to control and constantly nag . . . by using a positive approach, she can have a tremendous influence on him, which can change him. In other words, be positive, not negative and nagging all the time."
- "They seem very critical of each other. . . . They examine each other for flaws."
- "I would change the general impatience and dissatisfaction level. My spouse, for example; she complains that I do not make enough money, so I work longer hours. Then

I do not spend enough time with the children. Then I am wasting too much time coaching and Boy Scouts, I should be fixing the house. Then I am spending too much money on the house. This is not limited to my spouse; most of the women I know do this to me, my mother, my sisters, and colleagues at work."

Girl Talk

Many women will say "I'm just venting" or "I'm just processing." Call it what you like. To a husband, his wife's venting and processing sound like complaining. Let me give an example. Our neighbor Rhonda Rohrer has cut my hair for years. Yes, I'm man enough to get my hair cut in a beauty salon, which often has me spending thirty to forty-five minutes surrounded by women.

Because they know Laura and I deal with relationships, the ladies will sometimes pose a "question of the day." One day we were talking about the complaining factor. At first, all of the women were offended that any man would say such a thing. Then I gave them this illustration.

A man takes his wife out for dinner. He asks her where she wants to go and what she's in the mood for. Her reply is, "I don't care." So he takes her to a restaurant he believes she will like. All is going well until the salad arrives. His wife's salad has three cucumber slices; his, only two.

She comments, "I hate it when they put too many cucumbers on my salad." For her husband this is an easy problem to fix. In an effort to impress her, he offers a solution: "I only have two cucumbers. Would you like to switch?" Unimpressed, she replies, "No, you have Thousand Island dressing, and I like ranch."

Undeterred, he continues with Plan B. "OK, would you like me to have the waiter take it back?" Her terse reply sets the tone for the rest of the evening. "No, I'll just burp cucumber all night, that's all."

For a man, this isn't processing or venting; it's complaining about a meal that someone else is cooking, that is being paid for with hard-earned cash, and that is being cleaned up without the wife having to lift a finger. It's complaining. When wives complain, husbands feel unappreciated.

You Say Potato, I Say Potahto

Many of you may feel conflicted at this point. The simple truth is that men and women are different. She might think, *You can remember to change the oil in the car but you can't remember to change your underwear?* He might think, *You can rotate you handbags with every season but you can't remember to rotate the tires?*

Clearly, women consider the sharing of emotions a serious matter. But, ask any man and he will share that figuring out how to pay the mortgage or send a child to college are pretty vital issues. For a woman, wrestling with emotions requires deep thought. For a man, wrestling with problems requires deep thought. Both emotions and problem-solving are essential matters that need to be addressed in marriage.

The Heart of the Matter

It all comes down to whether or not we feel appreciated. In our survey, couples revealed over and over what makes them feel unappreciated. Women feel unappreciated when their husbands don't listen or share intimate conversation. Men feel unappreciated when their wives criticize them and complain. Throughout this book, we've given examples of phrases to use that will let spouses know they are appreciated.

But be careful not to confuse appreciation with understanding. God uniquely created each of us. We may never understand certain aspects of our spouses. The good news is you don't have to understand them to appreciate them.

Lessons at Apache Trout

Pete and Beth McAndrews are good friends that were in our small group of couples for a number of years. Pete is an orthopedic surgeon. Beth is a nurse who transitioned into a stay-at-home mom with their two beautiful children. It was a sad day when they moved away so Pete could take a prestigious fellowship with the University of Minnesota. When this professional opportunity was over, Pete and Beth settled into a new practice in Traverse City, Michigan.

One weekend, a number of our old small group was in Traverse City. While we were there, we met Pete and Beth at one of our favorite restaurants, Apache Trout Grill. Apache Trout is your quintessential Northern Michigan restaurant, nestled on the shores of Grand Traverse Bay. Summer dining on the outdoor terrace is quite the culinary experience. The ambiance is unmatched: great service, great views, and a lobster and shrimp bisque that will knock your socks off.

For over two hours our group of ten sat on the terrace talking, laughing, and catching up on life. Five women sat on one end of the table talking about kids, school, and friends. Five men sat on the other end talking about sports, politics, and work. I had the opportunity to ask Pete one of the questions we've posed to countless people as we've written this book. "If you could change one thing about the opposite sex—without changing the way God made them—what would it be?"

After much discussion and soul-searching, Pete stated matter-of-factly, "You know the bottom line? We just don't care." He continued, "Men don't inherently care about the things women care about, and women don't inherently care about the things men care about." He hit the nail on the head.

A couple of days later I shared Pete's comment with Laura. As we thought about it, we came to the conclusion that we spend way too much time trying to understand the opposite sex. We all have one ulterior motive: if we can understand them, maybe we can change them. If we get enough information, we can find a way to make them more like us. That will not—and should not—happen. We've been made different on purpose.

This book was not intended to help you understand your spouse so that you can change them. The commitment we've made to our spouses is not a commitment to understand them. The commitment we've made is to care about them. We should care about what matters to our spouses simply because it's important to them. We may never understand why it is important to them, and that's okay.

We've often heard it said that the opposite of love is not hate, it is apathy. Dictionary.com defines apathy as:

1. absence or suppression of passion, emotion, or excitement
2. lack of interest in or concern for things that others find moving or exciting

Long-lasting commitment—long-lasting love—is learning to care about the things that matter to our spouses. When we care, we scream into their lives, "You matter to me!"

Lessons from a SEAL

Marcus Luttrell is the author of the bestseller *Lone Survivor: The Eyewitness Account of Operation Redwing and the Lost Heroes of SEAL Team 10*. The sole survivor of a heroic four-man Navy SEAL team, Marcus tells his story in vivid detail. Ambushed by an estimated 140 members of the Taliban in post 9/11 Afghanistan, Marcus survived through unthinkable circumstances and has an incredible testimony to the power of the human will. Written between the lines on every page is the concept that these men were willing to die for our country because of one word: *commitment*. They had made a commitment to defend our way of life at any cost. There was no questioning, no doubt, no what-ifs. No matter your views of war, you have to admire that level of commitment.

That is the same level of commitment that a man and woman must make to each other when they say the words "I do" or "I will" at the altar of marriage. Too many of us go into marriage thinking, *How will my spouse fit into my life?* We put our own needs in front of anyone else's, especially our spouses'. This mentality flies in the face of the Purpose of Marriage (for more on this, see our book *The Spark*) and leads to countless unmet expectations.

In marriage we are called to put our spouses' needs in front of our own. We know this doesn't sit well in our Western worldview. But it is God's view. When challenged to think about it, we know deep in our hearts that putting our spouses' needs first is the true calling of marriage. This is a freeing mind-set.

Joy or Pain

No relationship—no marriage—can remain stagnant. Your marriage is either growing or deteriorating. It's that simple. Two words can help you assess your relationship: *joy* and *pain*.

Every thought you have, every word you say, every action you make brings a degree of either joy or pain to your spouse. From the smallest gesture to the biggest sacrifice, everything impacts our marriage. When we realize this fact, we can begin to filter our marriage through two simple questions. Is what I'm about to think, say, or do going to bring my spouse joy or pain? Am I willing to bring a degree of pain to my life in order to bring joy into my spouse's life?

Here are a couple of simple examples from our marriage. Even though Laura has grown accustomed to my "tone of voice" and can shrug it off, what change would it bring to our marriage if I thought about how I'm going to say something, not just what I'm going to say? Similarly, what if Laura curbed her public display of sarcasm when it pertained to me? Yes, I know it's simply her sense of humor, and I too have grown accustomed to it and can easily shrug it off. But what if she didn't do that anymore? How would that change our marriage?

In both of these instances, some could argue that because we have grown accustomed to our spouses' insensitive or thoughtless actions, we wouldn't notice if they stopped—nothing would change. However, we believe that the imperceptible change at first would invoke a dramatic long-term turn in our marriage. Most people don't realize that a one-degree change in a twenty-foot putt is the difference between making it and missing it. That one degree makes a huge difference over twenty feet of freshly mown grass. In the same way, that small one-degree change in tone of voice or sarcasm can make a huge difference over a twenty-year marriage.

I'd Take a Bullet for You

Most men—authentic men—would take a bullet for their wives. We would stand in front of a speeding car, jump off a cliff, or stare down the barrel of a gun to insure their safety. So, why not take a bullet in the following ways:

- Spend fifteen minutes a day in face-to-face conversation
- Hold her with no further expectations
- Play with the kids
- Help with daily household chores

Most aren't going to have to take that bullet or jump off that cliff, but daily death to self will win the heart of the woman you love.

I'd Follow You to the Ends of the Earth

Most women—authentic women—have felt this kind of devotion to their man: "Whatever my man dreams, I'll go there with him." So why not follow him to:

- His favorite sporting event
- The garage as he engages his hobby
- The couch to watch his favorite show—the whole show without getting up
- The bedroom

Most aren't going to have to sail the seven seas or scale a mountain, but daily death to self will win the devotion of the man you love.

A Final Challenge

Our final challenge is to remember that your commitment is to bring joy, not pain, to your marriage. The truth is daily death to

213

self is more painful than taking a bullet for her and more arduous than following him to the ends of the earth. This marriage adventure is not for the faint of heart. But now you have some direction. The simple phrases you've read in this book—lived out in humble sincerity—will not only bring joy to your spouse but will also grow the love that you both share.

Epilogue

You probably stood at the altar like we did: hearts and minds filled with giddy expectation of the journey ahead. Young couples rarely enter into marriage thinking, *This relationship is going to be so much work*! But inevitably the romantic Streetcar Named Desire gets derailed by the big Locomotive Named Reality. Fairly early on we realize a successful marriage is rooted in hard work.

When carefully cultivated, the garden of marriage produces beautiful, rich, and fulfilling fruit that is sweet to the taste and nourishing to the soul. As with most aspects of life, Scripture gives us a picture of how to till the soil: "Let us consider how we can spur one another on toward love and good deeds" (Heb. 10:24). How can we spur one another toward love and good deeds? The eight phrases contained in this book are not merely random clichés meant to embody a dream life together. When used properly, these phrases will create an atmosphere of mutual respect and appreciation in your marriage. In that environment, you can freely express your love to your spouse, in word and deed, fulfilling the commitment you made at the altar. Soon you'll find one good deed truly leads to another and another and . . .

Enjoy the journey!

Notes

1. Anne Moir and David Jessel, *Brain Sex: The Real Difference Between Men and Women* (New York: Delta, 1992).

2. Helen Johnson, *Don't Tell Me What to Do, Just Send Money* (New York: St. Martin's Press, 2000).

3. Anahad O'Connor, *New York Times*, March 16, 2004.

4. Leon Patillo, "Flesh of My Flesh," *Don't Give In*, © 1981 by Word Records.

5. Pamela Smith, *Eat Well, Live Well* (Lake Mary, FL: Siloam Press, 2003).

Jay and Laura Laffoon are gifted and entertaining communicators who have inspired couples throughout North America through their Ultimate Date Nights and Celebrate Your Marriage conferences. They are the authors of numerous books including *The Spark*. Jay and Laura have been married for twenty-five years, have two children, and live in Michigan.